What Readers are Saying...

"This book was such a blessing to me. The message was loud and clear, and your transparency was authentic and admirable. This book will give hope to those who read it, as you have many great nuggets in here. You are a great writer with wonderful skills to communicate your points by giving your reader vivid details. I love Jane, and I love the fact that God is going to use your testimony to bring restoration to so many with reappearing spots. Well done, John!"

—**Jim Duran,** Lead Pastor, The River Community Foursquare Church, Ventura Ca.

"I seldom read an autobiography that gets my attention. John's new book, *Stop Spot-Cleaning Your Life*, caught my interest and I couldn't put it down. Well-written portrayal of how God works powerfully in our lives."

—**Ray Beeson,** Author of *Signed In His Blood*

"*Stop Spot-Cleaning Your Life* is not an ordinary self-help book! As I read it, I felt like I was reading a suspense novel, wondering, 'How is this hero going to get out of this?' John's honest narrative of his personal, family, and business problems kept me on the edge of my seat! I appreciate his honest, no-nonsense sharing of how the Lord used John's Carpet Restoration technique to reveal a New Life Plan for him and revolutionized every area of his life!"

—John Ansberry, Former Pastor of
Pierpont Christian Fellowship &
Founder of Lost and Found Men's Fellowships

"*Stop Spot-Cleaning Your Life* is an authentically raw and truly transformational journey! John lays bare his real-life struggles and walks the reader through the healing process that ultimately infused God's love and redemptive power into all areas of his life. If you need God to restore what feels like is beyond repair, you want to read this powerful book now!"

—Marlia Cochran, Pastor, Speaker, and
Author of *Where's My White Picket Fence?*
When a Good Girl Doubts God

"*Stop Spot-Cleaning Your Life* is a beautifully written example of the miracles that can happen when we allow God to become our Wonderful Counselor! The process God gave John Gray to restore one's life will work for anyone and every situation...if applied."

—Pastor Tami, Author of
Glory To Glory: The Tale of a Hungry Heart

Stop Spot-Cleaning Your Life

A Guide to Restoring Your Life to
Radical, Clean Happiness in a World
That Keeps You Chasing it

by
John William Gray

John William Gray Publishing

Stop Spot-Cleaning Your Life

A Guide to Restoring Your Life to Radical, Clean Happiness
in a World That Keeps You Chasing it

Published by
John William Gray
(A.K.A. Johnny Done Rite)
Ventura County, California

www.JohnWilliamGray.com

Cover Design by Dan Mulhern Design
Interior Design by Dawn Teagarden

ISBN-13: 978-1523960026

Printed in the United States of America

www.JohnWilliamGray.com

Dedication

To my gracious wife, Jane, who taught me through example that not giving up on love, and all the love I know with her and my three incredible children, is worth it.

In loving memory of my Dad, John W. Gray Sr., my sister, Christina M. Luna, and my cousins, Christopher Meyers (aka "Tank") and Michael Meyers (aka "Lil" Michael).

Acknowledgments

THREE YEARS AGO, I asked for my wife's approval to take action on what I thought was wishful thinking and a silly thought—actually penning my life story. I didn't want to write and produce a book. I just felt like I needed to. I asked for my wife's consent, imagining she'd say, "Maybe some other time," and eventually forget about it, and I'd be off the hook for this apparently insurmountable task without feeling guilty about it.

To my utter shock, she thought about it for a couple minutes and then gave me the go ahead. I thought I was crazy for asking her and thought she was even crazier for saying yes. It suddenly occurred to me that my entire life had come to a fork in the road: God just opened a door wide and left it purely up to me to go through it, or not. What I didn't know is that on the other side of the door was the unspoken "cry of my heart": the restoration of every arena of my life to Radical, Clean Happiness.

Thank You, God, for *continually* leading me into *my* life's limitless jackpot and letting me lead others into *theirs*…

To My Family...

To Jane, my Pumpkin, you are the best friend, wife, and mother a man could ever wish, hope, dream, or pray for. If I were a woman I would aspire to become as loving, accepting, inspiring, encouraging, gracious, and as genuinely beautiful as you truly are. You are a direct reflection of the words *grace* and *mercy*. You are God's perfect gift to me that I know, with ALL my heart, I did *nothing* to deserve—this *is* grace. You also accepted me when I couldn't even accept myself or you—this *is* mercy. Thank you for being who you are and for doing life with me and giving me the opportunity to do life with you. You are my noble cause, my calling, and my destiny. For this, I'm forever grateful to God, your incredible parents and family, and you. May every word on these pages, each thought in my mind, and every action I take from this point on reveal to you and them how "I just love you, Pumpkin!"

To my amazing daughter Ash'Lee (aka Sweetie Pea the Great), for being my hope and light in some of my hardest and darkest times, for believing in me, for loving me, for trusting me, for affording me the time and space needed to not only heal my own emotional wounds, but to learn how to love you and become the dad I always wanted to be for you. May the second half of our lives on this earth be a reward to pay us both back for the first half. You are kind, intuitive, wise, inspiring, genuine, and a unique messenger that *will* realize a calling that is bigger than life, and I'm so excited and honored to have a front-row seat to see it all happen.

To my amazing daughter Melanie, for being full of grace and understanding through discovering just how imperfect and human I really am. Thank you for loving and trusting me and showing me what it means to believe in and love God and truly have child-like faith. You are humble, sincere, intelligent, graceful, and a naturally-gifted artist that *will* walk right into a beautiful, bright, and fulfilling life purpose, and I'm so excited and humbled to see it happen right in front of my eyes one day at a time.

To my miracle of a son J.T., for being the loving, confident, and super fun and popular boy I always wanted to be. Thank you for always being so true to who you are and for loving me the way I am—for being the example I needed to see that inspired me to follow my passion. You are loving, innovative, passionate, intellectual, and a natural-born pioneer with an extraordinary destiny ahead of you, and I'm so excited and privileged to watch it unfold *for* you.

To my wonderful walking, talking, preaching, praying, miracle of a mom, for modeling the transformation I needed to see and experience. That, combined with your prayers, your faith, and *all* of your Joyce Meyer teaching tapes, literally snatched me out of the pits of my own hell and catapulted me to where I am now—my personal slice of heaven on earth. You are the reason I wrote this book. You believed in me when I didn't— you loved me straight. I'm very aware that because of your choice to believe, receive, and follow Jesus, that He has blessed me, and your grandchildren, and future generations with the calling and purpose of walking in the hope, faith, and love *of* God. For this, I/we are eternally grateful to you and I promise to follow your lead all of the days of my life. You don't know this, but you were the first person in my life to prove that we all come to this world with a God-given purpose and we can choose to live it or not. The other thing you don't know is that your faith and effective prayers secretly became my fuel to write and finish the book. And your financial investment was the fuel that funded and produced it. Therefore, just like you, this book is a miracle because without you, *none* of this would have happened. Thank you for holding this dream with me, and for caring about the details of this book as much as I do. I love you, Mom!

To my sister Anna, for your love and support and never disowning me as your brother. Thank you for tough love when I needed it and for becoming one of my biggest cheerleaders. You, like Mom, *always* prayed a good life for me. May this book be tangible *proof* that prayer is *powerful* and that it *works.*

To my brother Andy, for being the kind of son to our dad and mom that I wanted to be but couldn't. For the first half of my life, I felt "out of place" and I longed for the peace, emotional security, and tangible contentment that I saw you model. Thank you for seeing the best in me when I was at my worst and for still doing life with me when I didn't even want to do life with myself, let alone anyone else.

To my Tia Gloria, and my cousins, Alicia, Joe, and Angela, and my best man, Paul, who supported and believed in me. Thank you for only wanting the best for me.

To All of My Past and Present Teachers, Mentors, and Coaches...

To those who saw and nurtured my spirit, thank you for your love and support. Pastor Gordy, Pastor Bill Gorrell, and my amazing marriage counselor (and secret mentor), I thought of each of you often while I wrote every chapter because each of you were instrumental in getting me to start *and stay* seeking God.

To Dr. Lance Wallnau, for helping me align my gifts and talents with my passion so I could start taking steps that are in alignment with my God-given dream. What I have learned since then and have written about in this book is what is going to help me stand on the shoulders of an influential giant—yours! Hint: This is the exact reason I personally gave you the birthday gift of those football shoulder pads on your birthday in 2011 at the "Leader-Shift" Conference in Pasadena, CA. It's time to get them out and get them on...because it's on like Donkey Kong, Dr. Wallnau!

To BNI's (Business Networking International) founder and chairman, Ivan Misner, Shawn and Linda McCarthy (Ventura County Executive Directors), BNI Gold Coast my local Chapter, and Chiropractic Wellness Center's Dr. David Lemons for originally inviting me to visit BNI. Despite my social awkwardness and how much I dreaded presenting and public speaking, I visited and joined the BNI Gold Coast Chapter in October 2001. My company Done Rite Carpet Care was flat-lining after the tragic 9/11 terrorist attacks. My business phone didn't ring for weeks and my cleaning schedule was empty. I joined because my business was failing and this wasn't an option for me. BNI didn't help me save my business; BNI helped me to restore it. BNI played a big part in equipping, educating, and empowering me, my life, and my business to thrive. As I reflect back on my very first BNI meeting, it felt as if my life and business were literally falling apart. Now that I'm on the other side, I can see that they were only falling into place. BNI and its members and faculty are like a second family who accepted, respected, and adored me more than I did myself. Thank you!

To True to Intention's Amanda Johnson, my book coach and her team, Kathy Sparrow (editor), Dan Mulhern (book cover designer), and Dawn Teagarden (interior designer), for making sure it was powerful and polished enough to make me feel proud and like it was Done Rite. Your coaching, editing, and book production gifts are a blessing to me and my business, and I know they will be a huge blessing to all of my readers, too. Thank you!

With All My Love and Gratitude to Everyone,

John William Gray

Contents

INTRODUCTION
The Need for Restoration

"FOR THOSE OF you who came to better your life and business, may I have your attention?" The sincere yet serious tone of the marketing guru's voice over the loud speaker instantly brought my mind back to the worksheet. *Shoot, that's me. He's talking to me!* I stopped slouching, slid to the edge of my seat, sat up straight, and listened to his every word.

"This particular process is what I believe to be the single most important exercise you'll do this weekend. I do this regularly, and there is no question that it has helped get me to where I am today. I know it can do the same for you. So grab your pen and worksheet, and I'm going to coach you through it."

Dang...right on...finally...it's about time...crap, maybe this is it! If it works for him, it should work for me...I'd be stupid not to do it. I anxiously scratched my head with my pen as my mind swirled with hope and ideas.

With the body language and empathetic tone of a brilliant coach, he started, "Where are you? And what is the current state of your life and business? No really, be completely honest with yourself. Be bold and blunt, and don't hold anything back. Take a few minutes, and write in your answer."

After what seemed like twenty minutes, but was only thirty seconds, my pen still hadn't moved. I didn't know how to answer the simple question. *What's wrong with me? I've done this before. Why am I hitting a brick wall?*

The trainer re-asked the question, "The question is...what state is *your* life and business in right at this very second?" His expression, deep penetrating eyes, and stern tone provoked me to dig deeper. *C'mon, it's not that hard. I can do this. Think!* Still, nothing came. This frustrated me. Out of anger and disparity, my mind shot a hopeless prayer toward the sky, "Please... help me, God." No answer. *Figures, when I need You the most, You're not there...now I'm pissed!* I whispered the question aloud to myself, "Where are You?"

"*The Truth is this...*" a still, small voice answered, "*John Gray's life, marriage, and carpet-cleaning business are well on their way to crashing and burning. In fact, they are almost dead.*"

The instant I heard this, I looked around frantically, glancing over both shoulders and then behind me to see if anybody else heard it. No one did. *Somebody is trying to mess with my head. Who was that? What the heck is going on here? What does that mean? How do you know this?* I looked for camera TV crews. I looked at Jane, my wife, who was deeply engrossed in her own writing. *Am I on one of those practical joke television shows?* I calmed myself by taking a couple of deep breaths and felt myself come back into my body. I knew I heard a voice, as loud and clear as the man on the stage. What's more, I knew what it said was true and always had been. I was in denial, and scrambling to fix the mess I had created in my life.

> "The Truth is this..." a still, small voice answered, "John Gray's life, marriage, and carpet-cleaning business are well on their way to crashing and burning."

The trainer continued. Raising his voice, he asked, "Where do you want to be in five years?"

"The life dream..." the still small voice started, *"John wants a happy, healthy...and loving marriage and a confident, unified, loving family. He also wants to be known and have visibility, credibility, and a full measure of influence—not to mention a thriving, successful, and profitable business."*

A lifelong, childhood dream was instantly unlocked and reactivated—true happiness. My imagination took over. The still small voice's answer acted as a perfect narrator, as I saw a clip of my ideal life in my mind's eye, seeing my wife and I completely unified, going on relaxing vacations and romantic getaways. Experiencing life together and loving every minute of it, surrounded by giggling, excited, happy, confident, and loving children. I was visualizing us being successful in so many different ways, in so many areas, making such a difference in our own marriage and the lives of so many others. I almost cried tears of joy and burst with excitement.

Finally, the last question: "Now here's the 'gold' nugget and the missing link...How are you going to get there?"

"Unfortunately, John will never get there," the still, small voice declared. *"If he keeps doing what he has always done, he'll actually die trying. In fact, if he keeps going the way he is going, he'll keep getting what he has always gotten—recurring life issues that haunt him— just like those "ghost" spots that he despises because they always magically reappear in customers' carpet. What has gotten him here (his ways and his truth) will not get him where he wants to go—living his God-given dream. It's that simple."*

My mind went from soaring above my world to crumbling beneath my feet in the same breath. I felt confused, discouraged, and misled. I tried my hardest to keep my eyes from tearing up. That, too, was a hopeless cause. *That's what I came for? Thanks for nothing! I thought I was already doing that this whole time. I guess the joke is always on me. I have Jesus in my heart...I'm a believer...I go to church... I have faith...I pray.... Where did I go wrong?* I wiped the tears from my eyes as inconspicuously as possible and did a triple-take to make sure no one was looking at me like I was going crazy or something. Thankfully, only I knew the conversation took place. Not a soul heard those words...nobody, that is, but God and me.

> I guess the joke is always on me. I have Jesus in my heart... I'm a believer... I go to church... I have faith... I pray.... Where did I go wrong?

This was the first time in my life that I ever had an extremely intimate and full circle talk with God, let alone amongst my wife and over 500 other business owners. It was scary and very cool all at the same time. It was profound, intimate, and in my face, and the part of me that wasn't confused and angry absolutely loved it. I was in mental, emotional, and spiritual shock. The conversation seemed surreal, and it made me feel undone. *No way! That was way out! Did that really just happen? I can't tell Jane. She'll think I've gone nuts! What the heck am I supposed to do now?*

As we finished the worksheet and day two ended,

my mind was like Jell-O, and my body felt drained.

We had a very tight schedule for the last day. We checked out of the hotel and got to the event. I was still reeling from the events from the day before, trying to make sense of how I heard a voice that seemed to know me so well. I wanted to protect it, savor it, and that left me quieter than normal as we progressed through the agenda.

I thought it wasn't noticeable but at one of our breaks, Jane asked, "Are you okay?" The look in her eyes was a combination of concern and fear. I hadn't exactly been the rock she had hoped to marry. As her provider and protector, I had failed miserably.

A voice booming over the loud speaker saved me from having to try to explain myself: "Attention! May I have your attention, please?"

Never fails...the boot camp is almost over...here comes the famous up-sell! Sign up for a year of business coaching—it's only $15k a year! Jane gave me the signal that it was time to catch our plane. She knew I might be tempted to buy into another last-ditch effort to save our lives.

"We have a very special offer regarding our monthly coaching club. We decided to discount the price for this year. Sign up today and pay only $10k instead of our regular price of $15k. Hurry, as space is very limited! Does anyone have any questions?"

When Peter said the word "discount," it somehow blew a fuse in my nervous system. *What a hypocrite! No way, are you kidding me! He just did the exact opposite of what he has always taught. How is he doing this? Does he realize what he's done?*

As I looked around, all I saw were people scurrying to the sign-up table. No one else seemed to think that there was anything wrong with the discount, despite what our mentor had always preached. Heated blood surged through my body and my heart raced as I raised my hand to ask Peter my question. Jane flashed me a look of disgust as I accepted the microphone from the usher. Staring at the bridge of her nose to avoid the look of death, I gave her my normal passive-aggressive reaction—an exaggerated eye-roll and a deep sigh that meant, *Don't worry. It's not a big deal! It's okay, Pumpkin...just head to the car and I'll catch up. I promise.* I was already on her bad list and believed I had nothing more to lose by satisfying my curiosity. She was already pissed.

My hands were sweating, and I had a bad case of the butterflies as I gripped the microphone tightly. Every muscle from my waist to my neck tensed up. "Okay, next question, who's next?" Peter asked. I could feel people failing to see my trepidation because of the thick haze of information overwhelm. I felt violated. *Just spit it out...so he can answer... and so you can catch your plane!*

"Peter, I'm confused and upset. With all due respect, why did you discount your price on platinum? That is the opposite of what you said yesterday, and what you've always taught us. Never discount our services."

He took a moment, staring at nothing in particular on the stage floor. Then he looked directly at me and responded genuinely, "We all have to make choices for ourselves; we all have to choose what is best for our business or life. What is good for me might not be good for someone else. I have to use my best judgment and so do you. I lowered my price in hopes that it would help you all." My tension dissolved. *Wow, I really admire how he responded. He didn't get defensive or make any excuses whatsoever. He just told me the plain truth. I'm impressed!*

"Thanks. Your answer helped, and I respect it. On the behalf of all of us here, thank you for all that you and your team do for us! This weekend has opened my eyes and has changed my life. I am forever grateful. Thanks."

When Peter identified his incongruence and accepted his truth, it opened my eyes to see who the biggest hypocritical liar in the entire world truly was...myself. *This facilitator is genius. All he did was tell the truth, and he's off, what I thought could have been, a large hook. How did he do it, and why is telling the raw truth so hard for me?*

That day, I had no idea that while I was developing a one-of-a-kind formula for preventing and correcting common carpet problems such as reappearing spots and soil-magnet syndrome (which will revolutionize

I had no idea that while I was developing a one-of-a-kind formula for preventing and correcting common carpet problems such as reappearing spots and soil-magnet syndrome, God was developing a similar one-of-a-kind formula to prevent, correct, and restore the reappearing spots from my life-carpet.

the carpet care industry), God was developing a similar one-of-a-kind formula to prevent, correct, and restore the reappearing spots from my life-carpet (which revolutionized every arena of my life). That trip catalyzed a life-changing journey for me. I finally resolved to figure out how to get those damn spots out of my "life-carpet" once and for all and how to get back to a "happy/clean life-carpet" and keep it that way.

Only five years later, I am happier than I have ever been. I'm enjoying my children, and they're enjoying me. My marriage is restored, and I'm actually having fun running a successful business.

Which is why I had to write this book...

The steps to live a radically happy life are unbelievably similar to the steps it takes to restore a carpet, and they have utterly and completely transformed my life and the lives of those with whom I've shared them.

I believe that we can—that we must—stop spot-cleaning our lives. Spot-cleaning doesn't work. In fact, in most cases with carpet and with life, spot-cleaning makes the problem worse.

Let me explain. Imagine someone has a "kid stain" on their carpet, and they just want to spot-clean it real quick so it looks clean again. What do they do? They do what practically everyone does! They spray it with their favorite spotter and agitate it a little. And Voila! The spot is magically gone, and it looks great. They continue on with life like nothing had ever happened. Then a couple of months later, out of nowhere, and without spilling or dropping anything, that darn spot comes back, again. Only this time it's bigger and darker.

What do they do? The same thing.

They spot-clean it, and it goes away again. They forget about it until it reappears bigger and darker than ever. Then they wonder, *This is a pretty stubborn spot—maybe I should hire a professional carpet cleaner to remove it before it gets ruined.* So they pay more than they should to have it professionally deep cleaned only for the spot and soiled areas to magically resurface faster than ever before. This time, the carpet texture is different. The fibers seem kind of stiff and feel a little sticky. The owners then think: *That carpet cleaner charged me extra for this area and it didn't help. What a rip off! I'm going to call and demand the company fix it.* The cleaner comes back to re-service it and only ten to fifteen days later, the carpet looks worse than ever and the consumer thinks: *I wasted my money on purchasing this carpet and cleaning it. I give up! I hate this carpet! It's no use! I'm only having hard surfaced floors from this point on. I'll never buy carpet again!*

I have found the same to be true with spots/issues "magically" reappearing in my life. Some of the messy "spots" that were created in my childhood and youth followed me into my twenties and thirties. I spot-cleaned with books, workshops, gurus, etc....but the spots always came back until God used a series of conversations and experiences to show me a one-of-a-kind 5-step formula to prevent, correct, and restore my life to

> Some of the messy "spots" that were created in my childhood and youth followed me into my twenties and thirties.

radical, clean happiness in a world that keeps us chasing it.

On the following pages, you are going to learn those five steps, and be offered opportunities to apply them as you read my personal story of uncovering and taking those steps myself.

It hasn't been an easy journey, and it probably won't be for you either, but I promise you—it's worth it. In fact, there may be times during the reading where you find yourself frustrated with me, feeling like the progress isn't happening quickly or dramatically enough. All of us want a magic pill to make swift, epic changes—in fact, that's what 40 of 43 years of my life was focused on finding—but the reality is that change happens one moment at a time, one decision to show up for yourself and those around you at a time. And I'm convinced that the reason this book has such a happy ending is because I did just that.

My recommendation is that you read through a chapter at a time. If you learn it, but don't practice it, it won't work for you. It's the same if you learned *how* to restore your carpet, but didn't take any of the steps, your carpet would never be restored. I recommend grabbing yourself a notebook to jot down your "aha" moments, your answers, and any inspiration you may receive specifically for your own life.

This is the formula God showed *me,* and I know it has been life-changing for me and everyone I've shared it with—the principles work!—but God may have even more specific steps for you on your journey. Be willing to listen to that still small voice inside of you.

If nothing else, if you walk away from this book with a more powerful dialogue occurring between you and God, you will be well on your way to restoration.

Apply a few of the steps, and your life will begin to change.

Apply all of them, and your life-carpet will begin to brighten up and reflect more of the radical happiness that you were created to experience.

CHAPTER 1

This Spot Came Back Bigger and Darker!

THE SOFT, SUPPLE leather welcomed me, as I kicked off my shoes and sank into my recliner, covering myself with my favorite NFL team blanket.

It had been two years since the boot camp, and life wasn't really looking much better.

If something doesn't change soon, I'm going to lose everything—the business and my marriage. But I don't understand. I'm working longer and harder, and I'm helping out around the house with the kids and cleaning. Still no results.

As I grabbed for the remote and turned on the TV, my sole objective was to escape the stresses of my life for a few minutes and just chill. It gave me relief from the constant arguments and disagreements that clogged the arteries of my marriage.

Finally, it's time to stop worrying about the mortgage payment, forget about the stupid bills, and enjoy some alone time. Ah, this chair is so comfortable. I'm going to watch a little 10 o'clock news, forget about life, and drift off...

"So John, do you care to explain all of these sex emails?" Jane did try to soften her anger as she turned off the TV and slammed down the remote, shattering it in the process.

When she waved my phone in my face, my heart stopped. *Oh shit! My life is over. What do I say? Come up with something. Think!*

"You are cheating on me! No wonder you're always out at night doing 'late' jobs. You've been cheating on me this whole time! How can you do this to me and our children?" Furious rage stormed across her face as tears streamed down her cheeks.

"No, I'm not cheating on you, Pumpkin! It's not how it seems," I pleaded pathetically as I sprang to my feet.

"You are going to deny it when I have tangible proof right here in my hands?!? You are a cheat and a liar! This marriage is over. I don't know who you are anymore. I'm disgusted. How dare you do this to me! And you call yourself a Christian? You're the biggest fake I ever knew. How long has this been going on? I can't believe this is happening. Why did you do this to me? Get out of here! I can't stand to look at you. Get out!"

I'm in a no-win situation. It's over. She doesn't believe me. She hates me. I crushed her heart and smashed her spirit. As I considered my options, I noticed that our beautiful, sweet, sleepy-eyed three-year-old daughter, Melanie, was now at Jane's side because the shouting woke her. Luckily, our one-and-a-half-year old baby boy, J.T., who was and still is the embodiment of the word "overcomer," remained sound asleep in his crib upstairs.

> "No, I'm not cheating on you, Pumpkin! It's not how it seems," I pleaded pathetically.

Looking at Melanie is like looking at a mirrored image of Jane as a toddler. Both are blessed with long, luxurious chestnut-colored hair with a natural hint of sun-kissed highlights, flawless skin with faces that glow, and big, round, gorgeous brown eyes, bright with joy and hope. Jane is the embodiment of the word "grace," and Melanie inherited the same trait.

Melanie moved behind Jane and clamped her cute little hands around the back of Jane's legs, as if she was terrified of me because I made her mommy shout and cry. I suddenly realized the terrible fear I instilled in her and how I had shattered her trust in me as well.

Stop! Stay calm and shut up, or I'll lose Melanie, too. I took a deep breath as I tried my hardest to keep my cool but failed. "What are you talking about? This is *your* fault, not mine! All we do is fight and argue! We hardly ever have fun or intimacy! If we did, this never would have happened!"

Melanie looked up at Jane and I could see that the disgusted expression on Jane's face visibly shook Melanie and made her even more scared and unsure of me. *Did I just say that? What the hell am I thinking? I'm digging my own grave. Stop!*

"Are you kidding me? You have the tenacity to blame me for what *you* did? Get out of my space. The sight of you makes me want to puke. Leave!" she screamed.

I resorted to my typical passive-aggressive ways and, as Melanie stood crying behind her mommy, I muttered pathetically, "Okay, fine! I get it. Go upstairs. I'll sleep down here and stay out of your sight as much as I possibly can."

She picked up Melanie and left the family room. As soon as she got to the top of the stairs, I took a deep breath, relieved that I was at least able to sleep downstairs. Ten minutes later, the sound of the bedroom window slamming open and the crashing of my personal belongings hitting the front porch startled me. Jane's rage continued, "You might be sleeping here tonight, but your crap isn't! You and the rest of your stuff better be out of here by tomorrow night!"

I just laid there quietly and hoped she stayed upstairs. I didn't have it in me for another encounter.

I barely slept listening to Jane crying hopelessly much of the night and awoke the next day praying that I dreamt it. *Please, please, please, let it just be a bad dream. I can't take another divorce. It will kill me. Please just let everything be fine.*

It wasn't a bad dream. It was my worst nightmare. I rose early because she left the house before the break of dawn with J.T. still asleep in one arm and Melanie holding her hand and walking beside her. As soon as all of our eyes met, Jane gave me a piercing look of disgust and slammed the front door.

As I left our house that morning to go to work it occurred to me, I knew things would never be the same.

> **I'm a ridiculous failure as a husband and father.**

I'm a ridiculous failure as a husband and father. I'm so stupid. I can't believe this is happening. My marriage is over. She is going to divorce me and take Melanie and J.T. Why should I even try for a second chance? Not even a miracle can fix this.

An hour later, I slowly pulled my private office on wheels, a Toyota Scion XB that's wrapped with my company's name and logo, over to the side of the road and put it in park. I set the emergency brake so I could clear my mind before arriving at the first appointment. Even though the original purpose for my car was to promote the company and use it for sales and marketing, it had become more than just a moving billboard. I rolled up the windows and turned off the radio. I laid my seat all the way back and let my body sink out of sight, completely shutting myself off from everything but my worst fear.

"Please, God, help me! What am I going to do? My life is a living hell, AGAIN. Why did You let this happen? This is what I get for asking you to come into my heart? This is not what I signed up for!" I shouted to God as the anger, fear, and sadness built to a volatile level. Adrenaline surged through my glands and my muscles tightened up with seething rage as I clinched my fists and raised them towards heaven.

"Do you love Me?" a still, small voice answered my question with a question.

"Yes, I do," I answered aloud, as I lowered my fists and inhaled deeply. The question neutralized my emotions and shifted my focus back to being on time to my first appointment. I started the engine up again.

What kind of question is that? Why did He ask me that? These and other thoughts whirled through my mind as I arrived at the upper-scale, two-story house. Passing through the gated entry and walking to the front porch, I lingered over the detail on the front double doors that were handcrafted and made of solid wood. I rang the doorbell, still baffled by the question: *"Do you love Me?" Why was I asked it?*

Before an answer could come, the door opened.

"John, I'm so glad you're here. I think I purchased a defective carpet," Mrs. Johnson explained, her voice rising with concern and frustration. "I bought the highest grade rug money can buy. It's only two years old and every time I clean a spot, it just comes back. I called the retailer that I bought it from, and they highly recommended that I call you, so I did. I've heard great things about your company. I hope your estimate is less than the other two quotes, and you can fix my carpet."

G-r-e-a-t, that means I'm out of the mix. My price will be the highest—probably be close to double the competitions'. That's sucks!

I had been to her house just a year before to quote her first professional cleaning. My quote was too high then, so she decided to clean it herself. In just the first few minutes that I chatted with this woman, I learned a good deal about her carpet—and about her. She loved her home and, for that matter, went to great lengths to keep it looking pristine. The lady had perfectly kept, shoulder-length straight blond hair and stunning hazel eyes, and was dripping in Michael Kors, from her jeans to her brown chiffon tunic. Her posture revealed her pride in keeping herself in top physical health, and the overall appearance of her house was classy and clean. She had a conservative approach and an eye for value, as well as the desire, personality, finances, and energy to accomplish a lot.

It's obvious she didn't listen to me, and she's still spot-cleaning the same way. I tried to warn her that this would happen. This carpet doesn't need to be cleaned, it needs to be corrected. A "normal" deep cleaning is going to compound the problem. With a couple restorative cleanings scheduled in a strategic frequency, this carpet could be restored and she would enjoy beautifully clean carpet for at least another twelve to fifteen years. I could fix the problems causing the symptoms, and she would fall back in love with her carpet.

I noticed, on the coffee table, a spray bottle of over-the-counter spot-cleaner she'd used. It was a popular brand that claimed to remove spots in a quick and easy manner—something to spruce up the carpet and make it look nice again in no time flat. To gain more awareness regarding other cleaning agents in the fibers, I asked, "Did you use anything else?"

"Yes, but they all seem like they stopped working," she said as she walked me to the laundry room. There was a small assortment of multiple as-seen-on-TV carpet spot removers organized neatly inside individual compartments of a white plastic cleaning tote sitting on the washer machine. Against the wall in a labeled place of its own was the home carpet-cleaning machine she used.

I'd seen my mother make the same mistake and waste precious time and energy cleaning our carpet when I was younger.

What if, instead of hiring a professional cleaning company solely based on a low price and then paying over $200 on a home carpet-cleaning machine along with $15-$40 per spotter, she invested her money in my professional restorative cleaning process that will genuinely transform her carpet's appearance and *maximize its life? What if her cleaning tray had the same safe cleaners I use, and she cleaned her own carpet with her over the counter machine using my restorative cleaning process? I bet she'd save hundreds of hours of stress and probably thousands of dollars in new carpet.*

But she had spent her entire homeowner life harming her costly rug—not helping it.

I'd seen my mother make the same mistake and waste precious time and energy cleaning our carpet when I was younger.

I'll never forget the day my mom came home physically and mentally depleted after working a second shift to make dinner for my brother, Andy, and me. She ended her evening by getting on her hands and knees with a scrub brush and a bucket of soapy water to clean spots out of the carpet before she went to bed.

My heart sunk as I watched her. *Scrub. Scrub. Scrub. Repeat.*

Many feelings welled up in me—a mix of anger, frustration, and sadness. I was only thirteen years old but, at that moment, I wanted to cry. And in the next moment, I wanted to rage.

Why am I so upset? I've seen mom do this before a hundred times. Oh, it's because they said she wouldn't have to do this anymore.

She had just had the carpet professionally cleaned a couple weeks earlier. The minute the technician walked in our front door, I sensed something sketchy about him that my mom and brother didn't. He was a fast talker and really pushed my mom to hire him. He reduced the price three times, and the main reason why my mom went for it was that the carpet was past the point of self-cleaning and we were having company over for Thanksgiving Day.

The carpet appeared dirtier than before it was professionally cleaned not even a week after that man had promised my mom it would look great. So my mom called the company to have them come look at it. The conversation was short and ended abruptly, "Sorry, there's nothing we can do at this point. Your cleaning job wasn't guaranteed." Click.

Even as a teenager, I was morally outraged by this. I felt equally helpless. *This is so wrong. My mom works damn hard for every penny, and this company just ripped her off like it was nothing!*

And there was nothing I could do about it...

As an adult this still outraged me, which is why I poured my heart and soul into my business. I believed I had a better way. Yet I knew this client wasn't ready to see the truth. After explaining what the carpet *needed* to get the long-lasting result she *wanted*—a restorative cleaning process—I let her know the cost. Her reaction was predictable, "You've got to be kidding me! That much for just one cleaning job! Compared to my other two estimates, your price is almost double! I knew there was a reason I didn't hire you last time. Thanks for coming out, but no thanks."

With the utmost respect, I shook her hand at the front door. "You're welcome. Thanks to you too, for giving me another chance at earning your business. It was nice to see you again. Good luck!"

Oh well, I tried. That carpet is most likely a goner! I mused as I drove off. I couldn't help but wonder what this lady's carpet would be like if she had just hired me to clean it last time and implemented my interim care tips. *The carpet would have no issue, that's for sure...and she'd only need a light maintenance cleaning right now. Let it go, John. Let it go.*

As I made my way toward the next appointment, disappointed with another lost job, my phone rang. *Oh crap, it's Jane. Why is she calling me right now?* I answered the phone cautiously, "Hello?"

"I want you and your stuff out of the house. I don't want you near me—or the kids. I want a divorce. Stay away from me!" she shouted.

The adrenaline rushed again. My heart felt like it was pounding outside of my chest. *Shit! She's still way pissed. She's not backing down. There's no way in hell this is happening. I'd rather die before going through divorce again.*

I pulled over to park and pleaded, "Please don't say that, Pumpkin. I'm sorry. We can work this out. I'll do anything. Just please give me a chance. A divorce is not the right answer."

God, help me. Please don't let this happen. I'll do anything. I begged for help as I wondered if He could even help, or if it was just a lost cause.

"Maybe divorce is not the answer for you, but it is for me! You're not sorry for what you did to me or to the kids. You're just sorry that you got caught! I want you out of the house ASAP. Just get out!" Click.

She's right! I'm not sorry for what I did. I'm sorry I got caught. How does she know me better than I do? I was kind of surprised, but not really. I wasn't mad at her. How could I be? The truth was, I was actually angry with God. I felt misled and let down. *I became a Christian to avoid hell on earth, not to revisit it!*

I sat in my parked car reasoning with the immature, victimized little boy of my youth that just randomly reappeared. I felt ready to give up on God, my marriage, and my childhood dream of a happy life, and go back to being a bully and having a chip on my shoulders. *I should've known all of this happiness stuff and God's incredible promises sounded too good to be true!*

The still, small, gentle voice finished my thought with a question of His own, *"Do you love Me?"*

I answered defensively. *Yes, of course I do. Why do you doubt me? You know I do. That hurts me that You have to ask me twice. Please don't ask me again. I love You and I need You. My worst nightmare is back. My marriage is over. I ruined my life again. I don't know what to do. I need a miracle, please...*

Then I remembered why I asked God to come into my life to begin with. In my quest for happiness during my twenties, I got married. Within the first year, things started disintegrating. So in attempt to keep the marriage together, along with the hope of happiness, we got pregnant, and my first child was born. My bundle of joy came, but the joy never took root. After enduring five years of a toxic marriage for the sake of being part of my little girl Ash'Lee's daily life, I knew I had to end it, so I did. I went from doing daily life and waking up excited to seeing my sweet girl Ash'Lee every day to only seeing her for eight hours once a week on Sunday, and it just wasn't enough. Not seeing her every day tormented my heart and my life. Sorrow and sadness caused my soul and body such physical pain that it became impossible for me to think about anything else. Every part of me was a scrambled, broken mess. I hated my life. I just wanted to be happy.

I was twenty-seven years old in September of 1999. I didn't know what happiness looked or felt like, or where to even find it, all I knew is that once I got it, I'd know it. I made it my personal mission to get it or die trying. Failure was not an option. I remember being so utterly desperate that I actually asked God to help me. *God, if You know anything about happiness, help me find it, please?*

The very next day, sitting alone in my very first carpet-cleaning van, I heard about His son, Jesus, through a recorded series my mom had given me three years prior.

The message was titled something like, "Double for all Your Trouble." The speaker shared what a tumultuous life she had and how God turned it all around. She exclaimed, "What God did for me He can do for you! Just do what I do and you'll get what I get— double for your trouble!"

At that point in my life, I had gone through a hell of a lot of trouble. *That's all I have to do. Are you kidding me? That's a no-brainer. I'm ready. Where do I sign?*

I asked God into my life at least one hundred times the first day. I felt like God unscrambled my mistakes, and I was given another chance at life and happiness. *This is it! Failure is not an option this time!* I wanted to do things right the second time around. I wanted a successful carpet-cleaning business, an ideal marriage, and an enjoyable life.

After a few years of enjoying being saved and experiencing the power of God in my life, I decided to pray for the perfect wife and marriage that I sensed He had for me.

A short time later my sister, Anna, set me up with her friend, Jane. They had worked together for years and my sister thought very highly of her. Before we met, we talked on the phone a few times. With each call, we learned more about each other. It seemed as if we had similar morals and values and liked to do some of the same things. She made me aware that she was Christian, fully believed in God, and then boldly asked if I was a Believer. That sealed the deal and caused me to ask her out so we could meet face-to-face.

Our first date was over a cup of coffee at Starbucks. Going into the date, I had no expectations whatsoever.

In fact, we both agreed to keep it to fifteen minutes and if after that we wanted to part ways, we would with no questions asked or any hurt feelings. The instant I saw her, I knew she was way out of my league. She had trendsetting chestnut hair that was in an up-do. Her complexion was flawless and further enhanced her naturally gorgeous face. She had big, beautiful brown eyes and a beaming smile, and I could just tell that this was who she was. She had nothing to hide or prove unlike every other female I had dated to that point.

Within a few months, we knew we were meant for each other. We dated, courted, and married about a year and a half later. I did everything I knew to do that could possibly insure our chances for a happy life together and a great marriage. We even went to premarital counseling.

The day Jane and I got married was the day I married up! She had a fairytale childhood. She was born and raised in the same house and by both parents. She went to private school and attended a Christian church her entire life. Her family seemed the exact opposite of mine. They were refreshingly functional, almost to the point where I felt out of place. In hopes of not messing things up, the first thing I did was ask God to come into our marriage so we'd have a better chance of success. It was at our reception as I said grace for everyone's food over the loud speaker. In front of over 250 people, some that I knew and some that I didn't, that I publicly invited God into our marriage. It was my way of showing God that I was serious about my commitment to Him and my new wife.

I wanted to do things right because I wanted His reward. Jane and I didn't move in together until we were married. Then we went on our honeymoon and started living and doing life together.

But the next thing I knew, all of the past "spots" from my life-carpet, that I thought I had long ago spot-cleaned away—permanently—started to magically reappear out of thin air, kind of like a ghost coming back to haunt me.

Jane simply wanted someone to talk to and do life with each and every day. Because I wasn't used to communicating while growing up, especially on a daily basis, I ended up leaving her feeling hurt and lonely. Not too long after we were married, she would ask innocent questions, trying to engage me in simple conversation because she longed for the closeness we had when we were dating, but I was far away—almost unreachable emotionally—even though we were newlyweds living in the same home.

> I wanted to do things right because I wanted His reward.

Jane committed herself to working even harder at being a better wife. She tried to be sensitive to my moods and needs, loving me as unselfishly as she knew how, only for me to come to expect these things and seldom express appreciation for them. This went on and kept escalating for over five years. By the time Melanie was four and J.T. was two, we couldn't have a conversation without it turning into a verbal showdown. She asked questions, and I became defensive. She tried to talk to me about her long-standing disenchantment with our marriage. Instead of listening, I made excuses for me and blamed her for the rest. I basically saw her but didn't allow myself to hear her. I preoccupied myself with growing the business so I could provide for us and make me feel good about myself. Things seemed to just keep getting worse with no end in sight. Eventually, over time these "spots" grew bigger and darker until they overtook me and decimated my marriage.

I did my absolute best to fix them but nothing seemed to have a lasting or positive effect. In fact, it seemed like the harder I tried, the harder I'd fall. I prayed, went to church, attended a life group, committed to one-on-one counseling and mentoring, read many books, and listened to countless motivational lessons. You name it, I tried it. I wanted to heal my marriage, but the spots just kept coming back. I was tired of getting punished for trying to be what I thought was a good husband. I finally became fed up. *This is a waste of my time. I'm tired of trying.* Jane and I were disconnected physically, emotionally, and spiritually—we were totally divided. There was no closeness left between us. There was only animosity. *I have no trust to lose. Might as well do something for myself that will be worthy of the doubt and criticism. I might as well make the pain she's putting me through worth it.*

> You name it, I tried it. I wanted to heal my marriage, but the spots just kept coming back.

I started secretly communicating outside of the marriage online, while simultaneously trying to be a good husband. Unfortunately, the more I tried to help around the house and help with the kids, the more turbulent the marriage got. So I stopped trying to cover my digital trail. I wanted to get caught before I got carried away and actually tried to meet someone from an online post in person.

Thanks for all your help, God. I'm over this. I have Jesus in my heart. I pray. I have faith. I go to church. I work hard to pay the bills. I try to help with the kids. I try to help more at home. I've done all that I know to do and none of it works. Your promise of "Double for Your Trouble" is like a carrot on a stick. It's a lie. The more I try, the further away it gets. I'm done!

God knew full well what I wanted. He knew I had been trying hard. He also knew that I was totally burnt out. I wasn't mad at Him. I was disappointed. *If You love me so much, why are You letting me go down this painful path?*

Sitting in the front seat of my car, I couldn't help but think that it seemed like He had me right where He wanted me—perfectly broken—being kicked out of my marriage and my home.

Then as He reached down to gingerly collect my brokenness into the palm of His hand, He asked again, *"Do you love Me?"*

This time the question affected me differently. It didn't confuse me. It didn't make me feel scared. It actually made me feel safe—important.

I vented my frustration: "I said 'Yes, I do' already. This is ridiculous. Of course I love You. If I didn't, I wouldn't talk to You anymore. You would be dead to me. Why do You keep asking me? You don't believe me. Why do You doubt me like everyone else? I'm over this! If You don't believe me, then just let me die already!"

My temper finished erupting as I sat in my car with a death grip on the steering wheel, like I was mentally preparing for battle, seething at God. "The double for my trouble promise is a lie!" Then like a knee-jerk reaction, I raised white knuckled fists posed ready to strike. "This is a bunch of bullshit! I refuse to go through a living hell again! If You are who You say You are, then show me! Prove it to me by keeping your promise to me. Resurrect and restore my marriage and life like You, and only You, say You can!"

"No, John, do you really love Me?" His persistence, sincere tone, and deep yearning hit me like a freight train. I could feel the weight of His desire to be loved by me. It overwhelmed, shocked, and humbled me as I saw His longing to be truly loved was so much greater than mine. At this point, I felt like I had lost everything, except Jesus. It was as if He Himself was asking me, *John, am I enough for you?*

I was caught off-guard. *Oh crapper.*

"John, you don't truly love Me for who I am. You truly love Me for what I do."

You actually heard all that? Are You kidding me right now? I thought You left after I lashed out at You. I'm sorry, God. Of course I love You.

"John, you don't truly love Me for who I am. You truly love Me for what I do. I want the same thing you want. I don't want to be used. I just long to be Truly Loved for

who I Am."

His statement was like a brand new, razor sharp, carpet knife with a laser-guided scope cutting straight through me and to the core of the problem causing all of my unwanted symptoms. The blade was so sharp and so fast. In the blink of an eye, I was able to see my entire life from a totally different perspective. It was clear to see that Jesus had never been enough for me. This new state of awareness put me into a state of shock where I felt as if I had an out-of-body experience. *What does that mean to Truly love? I thought I did truly love. I know that I want to. How do I do that? What does that look like? How do I learn that?*

Everything I ever knew about life, love, and God was totally undone. I thought I knew a lot, but it turned out, all I knew was my truth. Now I wanted to know The Truth. My desire to know The Truth made me question everything.

I started my car and drove away, trying to process the last thirty-nine-years of my life before the next appointment. *Wow! My life is a real mess, but really, it's always been. And it's not all my fault.*

I shook my head to clear it as I approached the house of my next appointment. The door opened seconds after I rang the bell, and I looked into the excited, crystal-blue eyes of a professional woman dressed in black pumps and a matching stark black and white suit designed by Ann Taylor. She had tightly curled, medium-length blonde hair and was bubbling with excitement, making the curls bounce.

"Hi! I'm so happy you're here. My realtor said you

help situations like mine all the time, so I called you! We had our carpet cleaned by another company two weeks ago, and they already look dingy again. This main walkway is the darkest area and was our original reason for cleaning to begin with. We have been super careful not to spill or track anything on it so I'm sure this isn't from us. I'm hoping you can make it nice again." The genuine hopefulness that coated her words recharged my energy to deliver the kind of result my company is known for. *All this carpet needs is for the pH of the pile to be corrected, and it'll be good to go!*

As I felt the confidence percolate, I steadied my voice and handed her the cleaning quote. Hoping to eliminate any resistance so I could correct the carpet right then, I added, "I can definitely help you. Your carpet has a very common issue that my restorative cleaning process will fix immediately, and I'm prepared to do a great job right now."

With a deep sigh of relief, she put the estimate down without even looking at it. "I'm so glad you can fix it. This carpet was expensive and it's only a year old. Please correct it now and you'll be the only company we use from here on." She relaxed her shoulders and smiled as she signed the invoice to authorize me to begin the process. With a measure of optimism, she said, "I'm so glad I found your company," and then left me to clean while she ran some errands.

As I looked at the problematic carpet, I shook my head, sad that a one-year-old carpet looked five years old because it hadn't been cleaned properly. And it wasn't this lady's fault. However, she took it upon herself to get it fixed as soon as she noticed there was a problem.

As I began reviving the carpet to its original color, I couldn't help but think about the messy carpet of my own life. It occurred to me again that my mess wasn't my entire fault, either. As I started restoring her darkest area of carpet, the main pathway and the initial problem, I flashed back as far as I could remember, to try and identify the original spots in my life that definitely were not my fault.

> As I began reviving the carpet to its original color, I couldn't help but think about the messy carpet of my own life.

The first setback happened when I was around seven years old. My parents divorced without warning or any explanation. I remembered it like it was yesterday. One day, they said they were getting a divorce, and on the next day Dad left with his clothes and car and never moved back in. *The least they could've done was given me a warning or an explanation or at least some kind of reassurance.* After my parents split up and until I became a teenager, anytime one had something to say to the other, they said it to me and I relayed their messages back and forth. It created tension in my young life because I never knew how each might react to the other's accusations or threats. What caused the most friction is when I lost my dad to another family and had to periodically request child support checks from my father and stepmother.

The next incident happened when I wanted to talk to my parents and try to understand why the divorce happened. I asked questions but they never gave an explanation. The more I asked, the madder they got. The angrier they got, the more the pain from their punishments intensified. In fact, the last resort was walking me to the backyard to pick a meaty branch for them to discipline my naked bottom with. They were nice enough to let me choose my own branch and decide if I wanted to be whipped with the leaves on it or not. Regardless of what I picked, the branch always ripped my flesh and I would have to clean myself afterwards. When that stopped working, they tried to scare me straight by having me pack my clothes and dropping me off at an orphanage. My mom would throw me in the car and then march me up to the door of the building. I was terrified. But Mom didn't go through with it. She came back for me. But by then it was too late.

The next predicament happened when I was around twelve-years-old. I was molested over a one-year period. My mom started dating and periodically hired a sitter to watch my younger brother and me. The babysitter, a 6' 2," twenty-three-year old male with brownish hair that looked like it was cut in the shape of a bowl, molested me a few times per month. My stomach churned just thinking about it, and I felt my jaw tighten. *Even if I had told my parents, they wouldn't have believed me.*

The first setback happened when I was around seven years old.

The last crisis happened when I was sixteen years old. It was a two-part time bomb. The first piece was my dad's death. He battled cancer for a couple years and finally gave up at the age of fifty-four. It seemed so fast and unfair. The second part was his funeral. It was at a Christian church. The pastor talked about my dad in such a way that I questioned if he actually knew him at all or if he was just blowing smoke up everyone's asses. He said my dad loved Jesus Christ and was a strong believer. That put me over-the-edge. I remember thinking, *If dad loved Jesus so much, why didn't he ever tell me about Him? What the hell is up with that?*

"Wow, it's turning out super good!" My customer's chipper voice startled me out of my jog down memory lane.

My mind scrambled back to the job. "Thanks! I think so, too. I'm so happy you like it. Boy, you sure can tell a difference, huh?"

"Yes, I sure can!" She gave me a reassuring smile and two thumbs up before turning and leaving the room.

I probably shouldn't think about my mess until I get done and paid for solving this one. I'll figure it out after, while I'm by myself.

Before I started packing up the equipment, I paused to look at the carpet. *I have to admit. I did a great job! Not only does it look super clean and bright, it actually feels clean and healthy. The pile isn't matted, and it doesn't feel crunchy anymore either. I definitely fixed its problem. This job was "Done Rite!"* The carpet was restored. The rug was back to an optimized state so she could maintain it from there on. I closed out the invoice and went to pack up the equipment and call it the end of that workday.

As I loaded the equipment, I wondered why is it so easy for me to accurately diagnose and cure the most problematic carpet, yet I couldn't seem to pinpoint and heal the reappearing problems in my own life. I drove away from the job thinking, *Okay, now what? If I go home this early, it will only make matters worse because my life and marriage are a disaster.* I drove to a nearby shopping center's multilevel parking structure and parked in a remote parking spot on the bottom level to relax and kill time.

My mind quickly drifted to what happened after my dad died. *I got kicked out of the house a couple months after the funeral, did drugs and used crime to survive on the streets, got sloppy (and caught) on purpose, went to prison, did drugs and used crime again to survive and make a name for myself in prison.*

"C'mon, Daddy! Let's go on the stair ride before it turns off!" The voice of a small boy talking excitedly to his dad as they approached the escalator brought me back to the loud echoing sounds of the massive concrete parking structure.

As I watched the father and son playfully hop on to the escalator and ride it to the next level and lost sight of their happiness, I caught sight of my folly. I watched carefully as the creation of my first and original spot played before my eyes in slow motion—my parents' divorce and their refusal to answer my questions. I was shocked. *No way, how can this be? I can't believe this! That's impossible!*

When I finished examining my life from present to beginning, I watched it again. This time, it played from the beginning to present. I saw clearly, with my own eyes, exactly how I used God every step of the way. *Buying my condo, getting me out of trouble, keeping me out of trouble, saving my business a couple of times, growing my business, marrying Jane, healing my son J.T.'s heart condition, changing everyone else but me.* I was appalled. *That original little spot mutated itself into my worst nightmare.* I had no choice but to believe it, because I saw it transform with every choice I made right before my eyes.

I knew that this related to carpet issues as well. This eye-opening concept made me think about the two appointments I had for that day. The first customer was impossible to please and on the verge of wrecking her floor. The second one was a pleasure to help and well on her way to enjoying an always-clean carpet with a long, healthy life.

Duh! No wonder I'm a mess. I'm pathetic just like the first client. I make excuses for how I act and blame the negative consequences of my actions on innocent people. I refuse to stay in this vicious cycle any longer. I want my life restored the way I restored that carpet, today.

> I saw clearly, with my own eyes, exactly how I used God every step of the way.

I knew how to restore a carpet. The problem was I didn't know how to restore my life. Then a harsh reality hit me like a freight train. *I don't need it restored. I need it resurrected!* It was obvious to me that I couldn't do this. But I knew who could— only God.

But I didn't want to use God again. It hurt me to hear it from Him, but it killed me even worse when I saw it with my own two eyes. It opened my eyes to see how I used Him and made my own mess. *I want to correct this once for all, but how? How do I do this without using God? I guess I don't know how to not use You. Please show me.*

"*I will.*" The answer came quickly.

And with those two words, I started the car and headed home.

CHAPTER 2

You Mean I Made It Worse?

THE AIR FELT bone-chillingly cold when I awoke and noticed that I was blanket-less and my back hurt. I tried to focus, to pull a complete thought together, but the uncertainty in the room hindered me. My mind felt foggy, and I hesitated to speak when I saw Jane's face.

"I want you out of my life and this house forever! You are a two-faced liar and the biggest hypocrite I've ever known! Get your shit out of my house and stay away from me! Don't come back here ever again! If you're not gone before I get back, I'm getting a restraining order!" she screamed as she leaned over the recliner I had slept in.

Believe me. If I could leave, I would. But I have no money. And nowhere else to go. My body tightened up with pure panic.

I chanced a look at Jane. She was enraged, her eyes filled with disgust and disappointment. Seeing her this way made me feel dirty, guilty, and ashamed that I was the one who caused it.

I don't have it in me to reason or argue right now. Besides, what are the chances I can save this marriage?

In a self-shielding stance, with my heart racing, I took a deep breath and tried, "Trust me. I would if I could, but I can't. We have no money, and I have nowhere to go. The best I can do is stay gone from home as long as possible during the day, and try to stay out of your sight when I am home. I'm sorry, but that's all I can do at this point."

With crossed arms and clenched fists, she took a deep breath and huffed toward the front door with Melanie and J.T. in tow. "Figures! But fine! All I can say is, you better stay out of sight! Stay away from me and the kids, and I want you out of here for good as soon as possible!" Melanie looked at me like she needed to protect her mommy, and J.T. looked as though he wasn't sure if I was good or bad. More disappointment and shame rushed through me as I witnessed the uncertainty in their expressions.

The atmosphere in the house was dark, hopeless, and suspect. I got ready for work and left as fast as I could because without anyone else home, I felt more depressed than angry. I begged God, "Please show me how to save my marriage without using You! I can't stand feeling like this! Will You please help me?"

I desperately wanted to fix my marriage. But I needed to know how to do it without using God again. I didn't want to use Him anymore. I only wanted to love Him the way He desires to be loved. This was my life's new goal.

I just need to know how.

"*I will show you.*" I could feel the warmth of His promise reassuring my mind as my spirit soaked in His words. As I backed out of the driveway, I begged, *My marriage is practically dead. I need this sooner than later, God. I don't have a lot of time.*

My marriage is practically dead. I need this sooner than later, God. I don't have a lot of time.

Normally it would take about an hour to get to the appointment, but all lanes were like a parking lot. *This is ridiculous! I'm going to be late to my only appointment of the day!*

Tuning into a Christian radio station, I smiled when I heard that the next show was focused on the ingredients of a successful marriage and was hosted by a well-known preacher. *Very clever, God. I like how You don't waste time!*

The pastor said that marriage is "no joke," that there are two keys to having a meaningful one, and that those keys require a lot of work: "First and foremost, you have to love your wife like Jesus loves the Church. And second, you must die to yourself and serve her. This is the surefire way to an extraordinary union."

As the show ended, I wondered if the speaker was actually sharing from experience or just book knowledge. Did he have a great marriage, or was he just a dreamer like me? *There was hesitation in his closing statement. Easier said than done. C'mon! Really, God. That's BS. I need more than that. I've heard this a thousand times from a hundred different preachers since I became a Christian. This is BS. I try to serve her. It's impossible though. She doubts, criticizes, and questions almost everything I do. She thinks I'm out to get her. But I'm not.*

This is BS. I try to serve her. It's impossible though. She doubts, criticizes, and questions almost everything I do. She thinks I'm out to get her...

I quickly tuned into a non-Christian AM station to listen to another show and heard, "Today, we're talking about the characteristics of a good relationship."

I get it. Thanks, God. I hear You, loud and clear.

The host and marriage therapist was experiencing a vibrant marriage, and I could tell by the tone of her voice that she wasn't all talk. She spoke about loving and serving a spouse in a similar fashion as the preacher. The only difference was she had tangible proof that it worked—her own marriage—and many of her clients' success stories. She shared the two most critical elements of a thriving marriage: love and service. The show ended as I turned onto the street the job was on, and I knew that hearing these two programs on the same subject back-to-back, with just enough drive time for both, was no accident. God was trying to show me something.

As I entered my customer's home, I felt hopeful that I was on the right path and that He would keep His promise and eventually teach me what I needed to know. *I don't know what to expect or how You are going to show me. But I know You will. Thank You.*

As my customer, Samantha, and I were walking over one of the darkest areas in the family room, I stopped and bent down to look closely at the surface, and then I parted the yarns with my fingers so I could see down to the carpet's base. I looked at the entire room from my hands and knees and noticed the carpet in the family room and the connecting hallway was in overall bad shape. It didn't look like a "normal" soiling condition for a good quality carpet like hers, especially since it was less than five years old. All the exposed areas of the carpet appeared very dull, even the sections that she never spilled on or walked over. *I'll bet money that ninety percent of this carpet's problem is due to improper care, not carelessness.*

The space of carpet she lived on the most had three monstrous eyesores which, to my trained eye, appeared to have metastasized and, over time, infected the entire family room and hallway. *I guarantee this didn't happen over night! I'm certain this carpet is done if she doesn't hire me.*

The three large, round blemishes resembled a large shooting-range target with a small bulls-eye in the center. Like a bulls-eye, each large puddle of dinginess, had a nucleolus—the deepest and darkest mark directly in the center of the blotched sections. And just like a target, there were multiple rings around the core that grew in size and changed in color tone. The darkest spot in each problem was at the core, and the lightest shade of dinginess was the biggest and furthest ring from the center that ultimately converged as one with all the others. The three dirty ponds looked like they channeled together to create a murky lake.

As I rose from my knees to walk with her and complete the tour of what she wanted cleaned, I asked her if there were any problematic issues with the carpet which she was particularly concerned about.

"There is," Samantha vented, her voice rising as her brow furrowed. "No matter what I do, these three spots keep coming back to haunt me! They just hide and come back darker and bigger. I hate this carpet! I have been disappointed with it since the first day it got a spot on it. I bought the most expensive one because the TV commercials convinced me that it was stain proof and would stay looking beautiful for at least fifteen years. The sales person I purchased it from swore up and down it was the highest quality and had the best warranty, so I trusted him."

Dang, I'd be pissed off, too. I wonder what she's tried? I got back down on my hands and knees to examine the particular areas she was pointing to more closely.

"Is the carpet ruined? Am I screwed?" she asked with hands on her hips.

I stopped studying the floor to look up at her, "Do you happen to remember what the original substances of the spots were?"

She sighed. "I remember them all like they happened yesterday. The first one by the front door is where the cleaning lady accidently dropped a plastic jug of liquid laundry soap, and when it hit the floor, the lid broke off and some of the detergent spilled and stained the carpet." When she pointed to the next one, a ray of sunshine glimmered off her diamond ring. "The second spot in front of the couch was from a friend that tripped and spilled soda pop. And the last one in front of the TV is some chocolate ice cream that I accidentally spilled as I was rushing to the phone."

> "Is the carpet ruined? Am I screwed?" she asked with hands on her hips.

With both hands together in prayer position, Samantha asked me a question before I could ask mine, "Can you fix it?"

"When was the last time the carpet was cleaned?" I asked, before answering her question.

"It wasn't even three months ago," her voice raised with her frustration. "I hired the famous carpet cleaner company from the commercials on TV. I paid a ridiculous amount of money for them to deep clean this rug. It still appeared dirty after they finished, but the technician told me it would look cleaner when it was dry. It took four days to dry, and it looked even dirtier than before they cleaned it. I called the company to complain, and they sent the field supervisor here to re-do the entire carpet. He was a nice guy and worked hard but the same thing happened. Within two days, it looked even worse than it did before the company cleaned it the first time!"

"You have every right to be frustrated. If this happened to me, I'd be fuming. I hate that this happened to you, but I get calls like this all the time. My company's niche is to prevent and fix problems like these."

Sighing with deep relief, she said, "Thank you, John. I appreciate that because this rug cost me a lot of money, and I don't want to rip it out any sooner than I have to. I actually loved this carpet when I bought it. It looked so beautiful and made my home feel warm and look nice. I'd love for it to look presentable again so I could keep it at least a few more years and start inviting people over again."

"I want to make that happen for you. It would help me a lot to know what other tactics you have tried, besides the last professional cleaning. What spot cleaners have you used? How else have you cleaned it?"

Samantha quickly listed her tireless attempts, "The first thing I tried on the laundry soap stain was an over-the-counter carpet spotter. It took it right out. But a couple months later, it came back a little bigger. Then I tried a different cleanser I read about on the Internet. They claimed it got out the toughest spills. It got it out, but it came back just like before, only this time it appeared even larger and a shade darker. That's when I got angry."

Her demeanor changed as she motioned me to follow her to the utility closet.

"This is my baby," she said, with a proud smile. "I saw it on one of those late night infomercials and bought it with the sole intention of conquering my carpet."

The home machine, in her cleaning closet, was pretty buff. It looked indestructible like a tank. I also noticed the utility closet was fully equipped with an arsenal of cleaning agents. You name it, she had it.

She isn't curing her carpet. She is poisoning it.

She isn't curing her carpet. She is poisoning it. I shuddered as the next thought hit me like a brick. *Like I seem to be poisoning my life...*

"The first couple of times it seemed to work okay. I felt like I was making headway. I stopped cleaning it for a few months, and it started going downhill fast. I knew it was beyond my level, so I hired the professional carpet cleaner, and I already told you what happened with them. Now my carpet looks ruined and it feels disgusting! It's stiff and crunchy. I'm embarrassed to have company over! I won't even walk on it barefoot!"

I had to respect her tenacity and tireless effort because she had enough spirit in her to give the carpet one last chance, even after all the disappointment.

"I just want to make sure I heard you right, so that we're on the same page. What I believe I heard you say is that you thought you bought the best carpet money can buy. But now you have second thoughts about your investment. And you are irate and feel like you wasted even more time, energy, and money trying to keep it as clean as possible, only for it to turn into a soil magnet, without you even spilling anything more on it. Did I hear you right?"

As if a weight had been taken off her shoulders, she threw both hands up like she had caught a miracle from heaven, "Yes, you totally did! Finally! Someone who understands my situation."

"Awesome! Now that we are on the same page, I'm going to give the prognosis to you, straight. What happened to you happens to a lot of consumers. The good news is that I see and correct this problem on a daily basis. And believe it or not, your carpet is actually top-of-the-line, and I'm confident I can restore it. What your carpet needs to get back on track is my restorative cleaning process. I'm going to measure the square footage and give you a written quote, with the exact out-the-door price, before I go."

As I took another walk through the job, making my calculations, I thought, *This carpet is not permanently stained and ready to retire. These fibers are just inundated with soap residue and are crying out to be revived. I know she'll love the way it looks after I treat it. I'm positive if she implements my aftercare tips, her carpet can be restored.*

I walked back into the kitchen where she was waiting for me. "Before I give you the quote, I need to disclose some important facts to you. Here's what I need you to know: The bid I'm giving you is not for a typical 'deep cleaning' like you will get from other cleaning companies. What I'm proposing to you is a restorative cleaning process. Your carpet is on the fence right now. If it gets another 'deep cleaning,' it will push your carpet beyond the point of restoration. With all that said, there is something else you definitely need to be aware of..."

Mrs. Smith nervously tapped her fingers on the glass table.

"You should know the carpet has complex issues that have been compounded over a period of five years. It doesn't matter how much you pay or which company you hire, it is impossible to cure a problem of this magnitude with just one treatment. However, if you let me perform one restorative cleaning process, your carpet will look much cleaner, and I will get it on the right track again. And if you let me provide a prescribed series of treatments, I can assure you your carpet will be restored. I'd hate to see you waste another dime on a method that defeats your purpose. In fact, if you decide against my recommendation, I'd encourage you to take the money you would spend on cleaning it, and invest it into another floor covering."

"Ding-dong," the doorbell rang loudly.

"The other company is here to give me an estimate, too." She hurried toward the front door and opened it a crack. "Sorry about this. But I just need a few minutes. And I'll be right there!" She closed the door and turned back to hear what I had to say.

"Whether you replace it or not, please feel free to visit my website and sign up to receive my online PDF Quick Start Guide that shows you how to care for it properly and easily. You'll avoid this vicious cycle forever and hopefully you can help others avoid it, too. This is preventable and fixable. Either way, I promise I'll help you! Here is your quote." I handed her the piece of paper and shook her hand. "Thank you for hearing me out. Take care, and hopefully I'll talk to you soon!"

As I walked to my car, passing my competitor at the door, anxiety started to creep back in. *Great. I'm off work, but I can't go home. If I do, it won't be pretty. I have six hours. What can I possibly do to kill the time?*

I stopped to eat lunch and couldn't help but spin in my worry. *I hope I get that job. I need the money. Please, God. Let her hire me. I know exactly how to restore it.*

Traffic was heavy, so I tuned back into the FM Christian radio station to see what show was on. The program was about what causes marriages to fail and other relationships to disintegrate.

I tried to predict what I thought the common pitfalls were. *They have to be bad communication, disrespect, not getting along.*

I was wrong. After the last commercial break, the host caught me by surprise with a key component that is common in every divorce or severed relationship. The common problem to every shaky union is *division.*

> I stopped to eat lunch and couldn't help but spin in my worry. *I hope I get that job. I need the money. Please, God. Let her hire me. I know exactly how to restore it.*

This baffled me. It made me think about my first marriage. *That's not true. The main reasons I got divorced before were broken communication, no respect, and we couldn't get along.*

Even after two hours in traffic, I still had a lot of time to waste before I could go back home. I was tired of being restricted from my own house.

After killing another thirty minutes, sitting in my car a mile away from my house, I felt a mix of emotions percolating. I felt angry, lonely, and annoyed. *Why am I giving up? Why the hell am I not going home? She is going to be mad regardless, whether I'm home or not. What do I have to lose? At least I'll be able to see her and the kids.*

Something inside my spirit convinced me to take the risk and go home early.

My heart was pounding through my chest as I turned onto my street until I noticed my wife's car was gone. *She's gone! Thank you, Jesus! Please, let her be gone the rest of the day.* I walked inside and did a quick check. No one was there. I got a snack and went up stairs to relax in my own bed.

Ah, I miss sleeping in my room.

I rested there for a few minutes, only to jump out of bed when I heard a car pull into the driveway. *Oh crap! She's here! God, help me. What should I do?* I knew it would get ugly if Jane caught me in the master bedroom so I rushed downstairs to watch TV. The tension in my body increased with every step she made toward the front entry. When she slammed the door, I could feel her anger hit a new high. She was by herself. I felt like I should either run or hide. But I did neither. I couldn't move. My body stayed in the chair, paralyzed by fear and helplessness. *God! I'm in trouble. I need You. Please, help me. I don't know what to do. I don't know what to say.*

She marched over to my chair, stood in front of the TV, and unloaded, "What the hell are you doing here! I can't believe you're here! You are the biggest liar and cheat I've ever met! I should've known you wouldn't keep your promise to stay away!"

If you would only believe me. If you could only see how much I truly love you. If you only knew how hard I've strived. To be a loving husband. To be a good father. To be a sound provider.

"You act like what you did is pardonable! You go out behind my back and cheat on me! You posted several different ads online. You communicated several times with God only knows how many sick people to orchestrate a meeting! I ask you about it and you lie to my face! You totally deny it! I show you the tangible proof and you make pathetic excuses. I call you out on the truth and question your actions, and you shift the blame on *me*! You aren't a Christian man! You are a pathetic loser!"

If you would only believe me. If you could only see how much I truly love you. If you only knew how hard I've strived. To be a loving husband. To be a good father. To be a sound provider.

Tell me something I don't know.

I hated this part of me. I knew what I did was wrong. And it went against everything I believed. I wanted to stop. I tried to quit. But I never could. It became normal to me. Eventually, I somehow convinced myself it actually prevented me from having a full-blown affair.

I always justified my exploits in my head. If my physical needs weren't met by Jane or myself, I fully understood that I had it in me to find another female that would, and it dawned on me that I'd have to file for divorce because I couldn't do that to me or my family. I drew the line there. That was the line I would never cross. I got married this time to stay married. Not to get another divorce.

My intention for the ads and sexting was solely for me to get aroused so I could release my sexual frustrations. It actually seemed to work, too. As lame as it might sound, doing this seemed much safer and "more moral" than a one-night-stand or something else.

It was my way of escaping my reality temporarily without hurting anyone involved—or so I thought. I figured it would kill two birds with one stone. My physical needs would get met. And, more importantly, it would detour me from developing emotional intimacy outside of my marriage. I seriously thought it was a no-brainer.

This had been a problem that developed into a pattern ever since I was a teenager. I remember being told by Sunday school teachers and all the other adults in my life, "Sex is for married people. Sex will mess you up if you have it outside of marriage." I had to date in secret, or else. I wanted to have sex with girls, but I didn't. I didn't want to disappoint anyone. Instead, I called adult hotlines to have phone sex, so I could satisfy my need. It wasn't my intention to break my mom's and sister's trust in me, crush their feelings, or skyrocket their phone and credit card bills. But it happened, and this was the final string that got me kicked out of the house and on to the streets when I was sixteen years old. The lust and sex hooks were set deeper while I was on a couple year vacation, incarcerated in a state penitentiary. It became second nature to flee my cell by visiting my imagination and erotic encounters to the point of arousal so I could release frustration privately before it mutated to public anger and frustration, which back then led to violence and a personal quest for power. I found that this habit helped me manage myself in precarious circumstances. I used it as an aid.

I couldn't shake it. I wanted it to leave me alone for good, but it wouldn't. It seemed to come and go and work as it pleased.

As I listened to Jane rant, I knew I had shattered her spirit. I also knew that everything she was shouting at me was the butt-naked truth. As I realized this, the loophole part of my personality couldn't help itself. *Oh snap! This is perfect. She knows this about me. God knows this about me. I know this about me. I might as well own who I am so I can finally be me. I have nothing to lose at this point. I'll finally be able to drop my front as a totally normal Christian husband.* I silently encouraged myself to go out on a limb and set the record straight.

73

Before I could even rehearse the words in my head, before I even realized the full weight of what I was saying, the raw truth seemed to flow naturally from my mouth as I rose from the chair to take a stand for myself—and my marriage. "I am a pathetic loser! I am a lying scumbag! You're right! I admit it! I'm a terrible husband and I fucked up! I couldn't help myself. I've prayed for this habit to be broken for over fifteen years, and it just gets worse! I don't know how to break it. I've been battling this most of my fucking life, and I absolutely hate it! I hate it more than *you* do!"

> I put both hands together in the prayer position as if I was pleading my case to God and her...

And then to my utter shock and disbelief, out of nowhere, it happened all at once—that "truth that sets you free" that the Bible talks about—an overwhelming sense of freedom, a breaking and unlocking, a shift in my spirit. It was as if those spoken words freed me from my life's 500-pound gorilla!

I put both hands together in the prayer position as if I was pleading my case to God and her, "I don't want to lose you! I don't want a divorce! Please, give me a chance. I'll do anything!" As I said the words, hot tears streamed from my eyes, pouring down my cheeks, soaking my V-neck t-shirt.

My sorrowful tears and earnest voice astonished even me because for what seemed like the first time in a long time, the words came from the bottom of my heart, and they actually seemed to penetrate the core of hers.

My genuine plea was the last thing she expected, and it caught her totally off-guard. She didn't know what to think. She was speechless.

As I looked at her, an overwhelming mix of hope and joy bubbled up in me.

The ten seconds of peculiar silence that passed seemed like ten minutes, as my mind flooded with memories of how much love existed between us in the beginning.

Five months after I had proposed to Jane, we mutually agreed to break off our engagement and ended the relationship (six months before the wedding) because a dark storm had encompassed my life and made me question everything. Jane didn't pressure me. She respected and supported me from a distance.

My forty-four-year-young sister Christina, who was perfectly healthy and energetic, was rushed to the emergency room because of a migraine headache that was diagnosed hours later as terminal brain cancer. Her life ended tragically soon after. It raised many questions to God in my mind, *Why stage-four-brain cancer? Why on April fool's Day? Are You just messing with me? Why when I'm engaged? Am I the butt of Your practical joke?*

Then the *joke* became a lot more personal on Ash'Lee's ninth birthday, the day my sister died. I didn't know what to do, think, or say to God, or anyone for that matter. I felt unsure about everything. That night, while at my house, I turned on the TV and watched the news. "Breaking news," the reporter stated with a somber tone as the news camera focused on a preacher laying murdered on the sidewalk in front of his church, with his grief-stricken wife and six-year-old daughter holding his hand and sobbing at his side. "A pastor was murdered today right in front of his church. He died because he was shielding his wife and daughter from the gun fired at them by a drug lord. His last words to God and his wife were, 'All is well with my soul, Lord. All is well with my soul.'"

I decided to stop trying to figure it out and to trust what I believed about God—that He is good and that He has a great plan for me. I thought if the preacher could say that on the last day of his young life, then that was the road I was going to take, too. *All is well with my soul, Lord. All is well with my soul.*

> I was able to see Jane as His good and perfect gift to me. We got married. I ended up taking the gift for granted. I didn't cherish the gift. I trampled it.

When I disengaged and turned away from Jane, it allowed me to turn toward God and fully engage Him. As I pressed into God through grief and confusion, He connected me to even deeper feelings for Jane. He showed me that she wasn't trying to change me like every other girl I had dated. She just accepted me for who I was. Through her unforced act of accepting me as a product of divorce, an uneducated and former trouble-maker, a risk-taking entrepreneur with ADD, and a divorced single dad, God showed me directly and distinctly that she was to be the wife I had been hoping and praying for.

I was able to see Jane as His good and perfect gift to me. We got married. I ended up taking the gift for granted. I didn't cherish the gift. I trampled it. And I had taken NO responsibility for the outcomes...until it was too late. There was no accountability on my part whatsoever.

Jane just stood there, only three feet away physically but miles away emotionally, looking into my eyes, and waiting. She must have seen that I was mentally distraught as the dots continued to be connected for me...

My life flashed before my eyes again, but this time I saw it differently.

I have always blamed someone else for how I feel and what I do.

In elementary school, I began misbehaving because my parents wouldn't answer any of my questions about their divorce. Instead of answers, I got dismissed and disciplined. I just wanted to know why Dad and Mom weren't married anymore. I wanted to know that it was not my fault and that everything would be okay.

In junior high school, I lied, antagonized, and manipulated my parents because that was the only way to get or do anything I wanted with the least chance of getting caught and punished. I was a good-hearted teenage boy, and all I wanted was to have a girlfriend I could spend time with like every other kid. I couldn't stand going to church and being an altar boy or going to school. It all bored the daylights out of me.

But did I really have to lie and do things behind their backs? I just wanted to be liked, loved, and accepted for who I was just like everyone else. Was there a way to get that without throwing tantrums?

In high school, I got bold. I began stealing from my parents when I finally realized I was in a no-win situation with them. My mom, dad, and stepmom didn't know that they couldn't scare me straight, although they tried with the 'orphanage abandonment' and 'desertion at juvenile hall,' and the 'leaving me at the teen-rehab center.'

I can see now that they were trying to get me to take responsibility for my behavior, but at the time, I felt unloved—and totally rejected...I guess I did try to do right by my mom for a little while—after I saw her sweating to get stains out of our carpet and crying after a professional carpet cleaner took advantage of her. I started helping to keep the house clean, so mom didn't have to do it, on top of raising me and my siblings and working one full-time and one part-time job. I guess I started to take some responsibility for my behavior then.

> **I can see now that they were trying to get me to take responsibility for my behavior, but at the time, I felt unloved— and totally rejected...**

And then when my dad was diagnosed with terminal cancer, I completely rebelled. I disconnected from my feelings because my parents, or anyone else in a position of authority over me, would find a new way to punish me for expressing them. I used addictive substances to deal with the physical and mental abuse that *life* inflicted on me. I didn't want to visit my dad. I couldn't face the pain of losing him, and I didn't know what to say or how to be around family.

But staying away and numbing kept me from spending a lot of precious time with him. My choices resulted in losing my dad without getting to say goodbye the way I wish I would have. Was there another way to deal with the pain?

When I turned seventeen years old and went on a self-destructive mission to finally take control of my own life, I disregarded all authority. I abandoned all of the morals I was raised with. I lied, cheated, stole from anyone, cussed, fought with anyone and everyone, abused drugs and sold them and tried to get others hooked, until I couldn't stand myself any longer.

Sure, I was in pain, but I knew that what I was doing was wrong while I was doing it. I also knew I was putting my family and many innocent people's well-being at risk. I couldn't blame anyone else but myself for that. Eventually, I gave up because I didn't want to harm another person's life. I just wanted to escape mine.

It was literally a do or die situation. I had been on a mindless crime spree to support myself since before I got kicked out of the house when I was sixteen years old. After multiple months of law breaking, it stopped exciting me and I became calloused. It started feeling like a 9-5 job, so to avoid boredom, I got sloppy on purpose and this made the newspapers.

WARNING: A teenage rebel without a cause is reaping havoc in the streets of Ventura. He's described as a handsome gentleman of a teenage criminal. 6'1". 185 lbs. Brown eyes. Brown hair. Tan complexion. Athletic build.

He's polite but we consider him armed and dangerous.

The publicity acted as a power switch that transformed me from a wounded teen to a troubled soul. My heart raced, my muscles tightened as I read the article. I was overcome by a combination of guilt, fear, anger, and sorrow. I wanted to shout, clenching my right fist tight and punching my open left palm. *Why did the article impact me like this? This is what I wanted. I wanted to make a name for myself. Why am I so upset?*

One reason, I knew, was that my mom started receiving hate mail and death threats from outraged readers, and I didn't want my innocent mom in harm's way because of something I did wrong. So I left clues, and this allowed the cops to learn my name. They couldn't find me because I was homeless so they pressured my mom and sister to work with them in hopes that I would turn myself in peacefully. It worked, but not until I had executed my last robbery earlier that day, and then had lunch with my girlfriend at McDonalds.

About half way through lunch, I noticed a swarm of police cars and officers rushing the place so I ended our date abruptly and evaded the cops. That evening I called my cousin, Joe, and he arranged a ride from my aunt's house in Los Angeles, California, to my mom's in Ventura County. My best friend and mentor, Paul, had been appointed to drive me because he was the only person big and strong enough to handle me in case I got out of hand. Paul was 6'2" and 235lbs and played college football at the time. He was a big guy with a heart of gold, and I aspired to be just like him. We became friends when he married my cousin, Alicia.

As we drove along the highway, Paul and my cousin questioned me, but I remained silent the whole way to my mom's and sister's house.

I walked in the front door of their house to see my mom and sister sitting on the sofa, holding hands and weeping. Knowing my life was about to change forever, I took a quick shower, put on fresh clothes, and warmed a frozen chicken burrito in the microwave. After eating my last meal, Paul—the person I looked up to, wanted to be like, and regarded the most—looked me in the eyes, and with a serious tone said, "I've lost all respect for you, John." His single statement devastated me.

Then the phone rang and my sister answered it and then handed it to me. A forceful voice boomed through the receiver: "John, whatever you do, don't hang up and don't try to escape. This is the Police Department, and we have the house completely surrounded. Please come out peacefully, and I'll keep my promise to your mom and sister that we won't hurt you. John, just hang up the phone, and come to the front porch with your hands in the air, and no one will get hurt." Click.

I opened the front door to a sea of frightened neighbors on the sidewalk, staring at the army of police officers and a full SWAT team commanding me to lay face down with their guns drawn and aimed at me. I went down without a fight, knowing I was just lucky to be alive and hoping it was a chance to pay the price for all I had done.

So the moment I turned myself into the cops was when I finally started becoming accountable for some of my destructive choices, I thought to myself as I looked back into Jane's eyes, silently begging for forgiveness and understanding.

I paroled just before turning twenty-one years old, and managed to fly under the radar and get discharged a year later. I went right back to drugs and illegal activities and found myself going through the revolving doors of different jails and almost back in prison a couple times. I didn't want to become institutionalized. I became cautious.

I finally realized I wanted to stay a free man, and that it was up to me. I knew if I had some responsibility out in the free world, it would help me stay out of the correction system. In 1994, I stopped sub-contracting for large carpet-cleaning companies, started my own carpet-cleaning business, Done Rite Carpet Care, and got married. I was young and it was a disaster.

I tried to blame my ex-wife for the way she treated me—make her responsible for my misery and self-medication—but I knew I was living the consequences of my choices. I just didn't know how to change any of it.

I knew I was living the consequences of my choices. I just didn't know how to change any of it.

When I was twenty-seven years old, I asked God to come into my heart and to make me happy, just a couple months before the marriage came to an ugly end.

I began feeling happy, but not happy enough; so I started going to church. Before I went to every church service, I intentionally got as intoxicated as I possibly could just before I entered the building in attempt to numb my feelings, repel all the people, and hide from the Creator of the universe. Sure, it was disrespectful that I went to church wasted, but I knew myself well enough to know that if I didn't get high beforehand, I wouldn't go in at all. My choice didn't make Him run away, and that decision actually resulted in me meeting my Maker.

I ended up experiencing the power of God instead.

It happened every time, without fail, from the minute the praise band started belting out songs to the moment it wrapped up the last one, I cried inconsolably, like a hungry little baby, and I always blamed the heavy flow of tears and red watery eyes on allergies. The last time I could recall feeling emotion at all was before my dad passed away. It was hard for me to believe I sobbed because I was always so inebriated, and because I still had the hardened heart and numb mind of an out-of-control substance abuser.

What happened next is what really burned my brain, even to this day. My drug high eluded me the instant the pastor finished a quick little prayer. Like magic, I instantly became sober and starving for any story about Jesus. I sat on the edge of my seat and took in every word of every sermon. I couldn't get enough.

I continued getting intoxicated every time I went to church for at least a couple months. Yeah, I knew it was inappropriate, but that was exactly the reason why

I did it. I couldn't put on a front and try to fit in. That's not who I was or how I operated. I went in belief that I was to give God a fair chance at proving Himself to me. My choice to go to church as I was—a desperate addict and a filthy wretch—ultimately resulted in exchanging the life I had for the one I have today.

I continued being loyal to my addictions and God until a miraculous event happened a couple weeks later. I went to visit my Grams, with the intention of hopefully introducing her to Jesus and saying goodbye, before she passed away in the convalescent home. I was nervous about enlightening her because she had never talked or mentioned anything about God or going to church my entire life.

It was on a Sunday evening, a couple hours after I had gone to church.

I got high and asked God to use me to lead my Grandma Helen, who I called Grams, to Him, just before I walked in to visit her with Ash'Lee by my side. My little girl was an 'old soul,' bubbling with ideas, wisdom, and excitement, and she bounced gracefully into Grams' room, her chestnut hair pulled back to reveal beautiful brown eyes and big, pinchable cheeks. Ash'Lee is the embodiment of the word "hope."

Even though Grams had Alzheimer's disease and was losing her life, her face never lost the light of her beaming smile. She was wearing her own pink nightgown and her favorite flowered robe. I was twenty-nine years old and felt awkward walking in because it was the first time I had ever seen her in pajamas. Her face lit up even more when we walked into the room, and my heart swelled with love for her.

Okay, I'm here with two purposes: to visit Grams and to hopefully lead her to Jesus and heaven. How in the heck am I supposed to do this when I know for a fact she doesn't even pray, or believe in God, let alone know who Jesus is?

Gram's question brought my focus back to her room, "So, John and Ash'Lee, what did you both do today before you came to visit?"

Ash'Lee answered for us excitedly, "Dad went to church, and I went to Sunday school! It was so much fun!"

"Oh, I'm so glad you had a good time," Grams said with a sincere and an innocently curious tone. "Tell Grams what you learned about in Sunday school and what they teach in church."

I was in awe during the conversation and how my four-and-a-half year old precious little daughter Ash'Lee was telling Grams how incredible Jesus is. As she spoke, Grams stroked Ash'Lee's medium length chestnut curls.

Is this conversation really happening? My grandma has never said God's name or even mentioned Him or church her whole life and here we are discussing both without even trying, really...

Confirmation came after Ash'Lee finished and Grams said, "Wow, this Jesus sounds pretty amazing!"

Upon hearing her say that, I took that as God's sign to me and I asked her a simple question that, until that time, I had never asked anyone.

"Gram, Would you like me to introduce you to Him? Would you like to invite Him into your heart?"

"John," she said, looking into my eyes. "Yes, I want Jesus to come into my heart."

Did I really have to get high before I visited her, or for God to use me? Of course I didn't. The reason I went there stoned was because that was normal to me. Plus, I was nervous about talking to my dying Grams about a subject we had never discussed before.

I couldn't believe He used me while I was under the influence. As I put the contraband away for the night, I divulged my peculiar truth to God.

"I love You, and I also love the drugs," I admitted, sitting at my kitchen table. "And I'm not going to stop. I couldn't stop even if I wanted to. And the truth of the matter is that I don't want to. It's going to take a miracle to break the addiction off of me. If You want me to stop, then You're going to have to make it happen because I definitely will not."

> "I love You, and I also love the drugs," I admitted.

My choice to not hold anything back resulted in me feeling better about my relationship with God because I was totally honest with Him. He made me feel like it was totally okay to just be me with Him.

After I woke up the next day and got high, I thought about how God used me despite the fact I wasn't sober, and the guilt about my substance abuse problem grew. *If God can use me in that powerful of a way when I'm high, how much more would He use me if I wasn't an addict?*

Later that morning, while I was at work, I learned that Grams had passed away. I felt sad that she died, but grateful that God used me in such a special way. As the day progressed, I noticed I had less of a hankering to get high. I didn't think anything of it because I was enthralled with the fact that God used me to get Grams to heaven the day before she died, and I started becoming excited because I sensed that was only the beginning of much bigger things to come.

The following day, I overslept and rushed to work, forgetting to get high that morning, and I had no desire for it in the afternoon or later that evening. I stopped doing drugs that day against my will and without even trying. I never got sick or had a side effect. The cravings vanished overnight. It was an absolute miracle. I feared and revered His power. How could I not?

Unfortunately, that set the tone of my expectation for our relationship. I would express my desires and helplessness, ask Him to help, and then He would help... and I continued to live without true accountability.

After He bailed me out of a major run-in with the law, I spent $2K to go to a business-building event to focus on the carpet-cleaning business and keep myself out of trouble. With the profits, I bought a condo and started dating girls from church. I knew I wanted God's blessing on my life and started feeling like I wanted to be married again, too. So, I started dating with the intention of meeting a woman that I would love to do the rest of my life with. I met Jane just before I turned thirty-one years old and married her eighteen months later. She moved into my condo and we started doing life together.

I made a personal goal to have a successful business and happy life. My choice resulted in me chasing the dream...and drifting from God.

I decided to rent out the condo and buy a big house and had to start working a lot more because the mortgage was $5K a month. Eventually, we began arguing over financial matters. She had seen the red lights even before I took out a large mortgage on the house, but I didn't listen to her. In fact, I discounted her perspective and dismissed her opinions. The more money we needed to make ends meet, the more I worked. The more hours I labored, the more we quarreled. The more we would argue, the more I'd stay away. The more I wasn't home, the more I lost my connection with her and the kids.

> My choice resulted in me chasing the dream... and drifting from God.

I felt as though I was getting punished for trying. All we did was argue and grow further apart, and the trust we once shared had disintegrated. I figured if I was going to get penalized for something I wasn't responsible for, I might as well do something that would deserve the chastisement I was getting, which is the exact reason why I started posting personal ads.

"John..." Jane's desperate whisper almost brought me back to the room.

It's no wonder why my life and marriage are a catastrophic mess. I made all of my decisions based on obtaining the life I dreamed of. I only did things that I thought would get me a step closer to my target, but failed to see how they were destroying what I really craved. Eventually, this created mess upon mess as I tried to clean the spots up, and I always went to God to bail me out. But I'm the one who devastated dreams and reduced my family's trust in me to rubble.

"Yes, John." the still, small voice came through. "It's your lack of accountability that has turned your whole life into something that resembles Samantha's carpet—a muddled mess of spots that you have tried to clean up with blame or, in your good moments, kinder words and behavior. But if you don't deal with the real issues and become accountable for your words and behaviors, you'll never get your life's carpet clean again."

> "It's your lack of accountability that has turned your whole life into something that resembles a muddled mess of spots that you have tried to clean up with blame or, in your good moments, kinder words and behavior."

I'm getting what I deserve. I'm going to go through another living hell. I'm going to lose everything.

The sound of my wife sobbing jarred me back to the living room with her. I suddenly realized that this was really happening. Something had shifted, and I really heard her when she spoke, "I don't know who you are or what to believe anymore. You are sick. You need help. I don't trust you anymore. I don't know what to say. Our marriage needs help. If you want to stay married, we have to tell Pastor about this. I want his guidance."

"I agree our marriage needs help, and we need Pastor's counseling. I'm willing to do whatever it takes to turn us around. I won't let you down, I promise!" I grabbed her hand.

As she left the room, and the constructive exchange ended, I knew without doubt that God was holding in His left hand all the pieces to my broken dreams, and had just used His right hand to put the first piece in its proper place. I couldn't help but smile.

God. You are my hero! Thank You! I'm getting a second chance! I know this is You! I know You made this happen! I know You are helping me. I just know it! This is what You meant when You said you didn't want me to use You anymore, right? You wanted me to see MY PART in all of this and step up and own some of this stuff instead of just asking You to fix it?

"Now you're getting it."

Yes, I am. Game on!

CHAPTER 3
That's It! It's on Like Donkey Kong!

"I HATE YOU," she professed through her own tears, her voice escalating quickly. "I don't trust you! I'll never trust you again! I'm fooling myself if I think marriage counseling is going to fix this! I wish I never married you! I want this to be over!" Forcing back the rage, she slammed the door as we walked out of the counselor's office and took off in her car.

My heart sank.

The first two years we went to marriage counseling, it felt like we were in the perfect storm. Anything that could have gone wrong did. Every visit opened up a brand new can of worms. Many trivial spots from the first couple years of our marriage, which I thought were totally taken care of, somehow magically resurfaced bigger, darker, and murkier than ever. Minor specks, ranging from an old spiff that stemmed from me not putting my stupid dirty socks in the clothes hamper, to a little more disgruntled mark that came as a result of not pre-planning whose family we spent our last Thanksgiving Day with, continued to haunt me regardless of how darn careful I was.

On top of the marital problems we had, we had also taken many financial blows. Business slowed down even more, to the point that I couldn't afford to pay the mortgage and other important bills. The risky, uncalculated decisions I had made in the not so distant past had come back to sink us. I was drowning in debt. I declared bankruptcy, and our home went into foreclosure. We barely had enough cash for food and gasoline, let alone the marriage counseling that didn't seem to be helping. The collection calls and letters from banks and credit card companies took a serious toll on us as well.

I took every bit of the therapist's advice and recommendations, and went above and beyond by reading books about being a better husband so I could love Jane like Jesus loves the church. I even occasionally read the Bible, prayed, and went to church more. Nothing worked. Regardless of what I did or didn't do, the carpet of my life and marriage developed a common ailment that I cured on a regular basis for over 50% of my first-time carpet-cleaning customers—a condition I refer to as Soil Magnet Syndrome.

On a personal level, I tried every approach our therapist mentioned until I exhausted the arsenal of tactics I had gained, much like my clients' exhausted use of multiple spot cleaners, companies, and home-carpet machines. In the end, I was exasperated and depleted.

The day my wife found the sale date notice for our home taped to the front door was the day I crumbled.

It was a depressing day altogether. There were no appointments scheduled. Out of desperation, I jumped into action and began calling past clients, and some potential clients with whom I'd completed estimates.

> The day my wife found the sale date notice for our home taped to the front door was the day I crumbled.

I left countless voice messages for people who did not pick up and endured rejection from the ones that answered. It also happened to be on Wednesday, our marriage counseling day, and just before our appointment. That particular session was very heated. It was like a bomb of poop exploded in that office and no one, not even the shrink, could have stopped it.

She hates me...

In just the few seconds it took her to say what a loser husband and father she thought I was, I realized her heart was still bleeding from how deeply I had wounded it. Any form of trust we ever had was destroyed.

Yet, I was determined that my marriage still had a chance. I quickly came to realize that it would take more than prayer, going to church, and marriage counseling to love her in such a way that she actually felt genuinely loved and cherished.

"Is this what I get for trying? This is bull crap! C'mon, God! It's over!" I shouted aloud, as I parked in my driveway.

"Trust Me. You're in good hands. I will show you," the still small voice assured me.

Then my cell phone rang, just as I was about to go into the house. It was Samantha with the name brand, high-quality carpet that looked like a murky lake.

"Hi, I'm returning your call from earlier today," she said, her voice a little vulnerable. "I never did clean or replace my carpet. I was too scared. I got three different estimates, and they are all across the board. I'm calling because you said my carpet was restorable and you stood behind your restorative cleaning process. I need your help."

Now here's a woman who gets it! Good for her! She is doing something about that mess—calling in an expert who knows what they're doing.

"I'd love to treat your carpet and coach you how to care for it!"

As I pushed the red button to end the call, it hit me. *Duh! I need to do exactly what that smart lady did! I need to find and get help from someone that can actually help me. Someone I admire and can relate to. Someone who is where I want to be in life and who can show me how to get there.* I tapped my fingers on the steering wheel as I let my mind wander to who could help. *Oh, I know! That preacher entrepreneur. He seemed like the real deal—someone who would understand all of the areas of my life.*

I immediately enrolled myself into a business leadership course put on by a preacher turned ultra successful entrepreneur who I'd heard speak at a seminar. I liked, trusted, and respected the Christian teacher, Dr. Lance Wallnau. He spoke with great charisma and I admired the measure of credibility and influence he carried, as well as his down-to-earth manner. He had what I wanted—a strong thriving marriage and a confident, happy, and loving family unit as well as a super successful business.

The curriculum focused on leadership and personality styles combined with business mastery, and the goal was to help us to become pre-eminent in our field of business or career.

I designated my usual alone time in the infamous recliner, while everyone else was asleep, to studying. The first question asked me to describe the current state of my life and how I got there.

I am a pathetic disaster. I can't stand coming home after work. My wife cringes at the site of me. I'm distant from my kids. When my four-year-old daughter, Melanie, draws a picture of our family together, I'm off in the distance, not even close to the family. And it's my fault. I act like a victim. I am stuck in my ways. I shift blame. I make excuses. I am insecure. I am defensive. I don't trust. I am a hypocrite. I'm insensitive. I'm selfish. I'm stubborn. I feel inadequate. I'm scared of rejection. I'm scared of criticism. I try to avoid strife. I get what I get because I do what I do and refuse to be accountable.

I am a pathetic disaster. I can't stand coming home after work.

As I looked at my answer and the very ugly spots in my life, I thought about the conversations I'd been having with God lately. *Jesus may have saved my soul, but He isn't fixing my life for me.*

Everything finally clicked.

It's no wonder. I get it now. This is why I treat people the way I do. Why I am cold as ice. Why I check out emotionally. Why I finger point. Why I dredge up the past. Why I push people away. Why I ignore. Why I can't communicate properly. Why I shut down. Why I am so defensive. Why I always have to be right. Why I have a controlling personality. Why I am bitter. Why I harbor resentment. Why I don't trust. Why I block people and feelings out. Why I question everyone. Why my life is in the state it is.

I lacked self-awareness, accountability, and right action. I lived in a constant state of reaction. I was never properly informed to make wise decisions, and I had no effective strategy for managing my emotions or feelings. In fact, it was quite the opposite—I let my feelings and emotions dictate my choices and behaviors. It's what I knew and how I lived my whole life, because it felt totally normal to me.

This is the habit that led me into the vicious cycle to begin with, and the trap that kept me locked in it for over twenty-five damn years.

A combination of humiliation, remorse, and embarrassment bubbled inside of me.

Well, I took action, but it was action without accountability…it was unconscious reaction because I didn't know how to deal with how I was feeling.

When I spot-cleaned the permanent stains of my dad's terminal cancer, I looked rebellious, fearless, and bold, but the reason I went off the deep end was that I was weak, helpless, and injured and it was the easy way out for me. I didn't know how to deal with that type of emotion, so instead of acknowledging my fear of feeling grief, sorrow, loss, and heartache, I tried to sweep it all under my life's carpet by resisting it. I couldn't keep these feelings from re-surfacing, so I detached mentally, physically, and emotionally from my dad, my family, God, and my life. Doing that created an even darker mark and so in an attempt to spot-clean that mark, I did drugs. The drugs covered

This is the habit that led me into the vicious cycle to begin with, and the trap that kept me locked in it for over twenty-five damn years.

the festering sores of my unresolved emotions, but they kept reappearing. I became desperate. I wanted to be taken out of my misery.

God saved me from my death wish and gave me the gift of time in the state penitentiary.

With my sentence to the correctional system at seventeen years old, I was just a kid entering into a man's world—Maximum Security State Prison. I spot cleaned my low self-esteem and trepidation with a new quest for power. I knew I had to take my game up a notch if I was going to last while I was locked up. My goal, while being incarcerated, was to make a name for myself and thrive, not just survive. For that to happen, I needed respect, power, and influence. In my quest for recognition, I sketched out plans that in my right mind, I never ever would have thought of, let alone executed.

Whew. I did take massive action, didn't I? I leaned my head back in the recliner and let my thoughts drift back to that time.

The first step, which I truly regret and am embarrassed to admit, was pretending to be a devil worshiper to force my Catholic cellmate permanently out of the cell. I made up bogus sayings and pretended to chant. I covered my cell walls and door with dark evil graffiti. I tore pages out of my cellmate's Bible and shredded them right in front of him. He was terrified and out in less than two hours, and word got around the cellblocks even faster. I took the second step when I stood my ground after another inmate, higher in the ranks of respect, had made an untrue and impolite comment about me. He saw it as disrespecting me and thought he called my bluff. I saw it as an opportunity to take his recognition and gain more respect. I jumped him. This landed me in the "hole" for many weeks, and I came out of solitary confinement more hardened. However, as I finished the jail sentence, my need for power decreased and my hunger for love and happiness magically reappeared.

My quest for strength ended, and a mission to cure the initial spots on my life's carpet—my heart's desire to feel happy and be loved—began.

> **My quest for strength ended, and a mission to cure the initial spots on my life's carpet—my heart's desire to feel happy and be loved—began.**

I first spot-cleaned the desire for love and happiness with what I thought was good and normal, with topical brush-the-dirt-off-surface cleansers like substance abuse, music, and girls. When I got bored with them, I mixed crime back into the picture to spice it up. The normal marks of loneliness and anger appeared to go away, but within a short period of time, they came back larger and uglier than before. After going back in and out of jail, I finally realized that I didn't want to make a life of it. I had to become a little more responsible. I figured I could kill three birds—my freedom, happiness, and love—with one stone: starting a family.

Eyes closed, I shook my head in wonderment that it had ever seemed like a good idea to me.

What a disaster. I ended up hurting everyone involved.

I took action, again, but it was reactive. What is it that makes an action 'right' for me? I mean, I understand owning my part of it now, but how do I know if I'm acting and not reacting?

I started the next lesson and grinned from ear-to-ear when he said, "This is about creating the life you most want. The people most successful in these studies focused on giant and more long-term goals which, as a result of their size, included service and helping others." As he discussed the typical mindset of the average decision-maker, who set their sights on commonplace shorter-termed objectives, I almost finished his thought before he said it out loud, "Their aim is only in serving themselves."

Whew. All of those actions I took were for me, and me alone. I tried to protect myself from the pain of losing my dad. I acted like a prick in prison to earn power and respect...to protect myself. And then I got married... to experience love and happiness...to protect myself from being lonely and ending up in jail forever. Wow. That's what that life-sentence threat was all about— God showing me that I didn't have to react to protect myself anymore.

When I was twenty-eight-and-a-half years old, I was accused of a violent crime that I didn't commit. I was charged with a felony, and was facing a possible life-sentence. I was pissed-off at God. Yet from the minute I got booked into county jail to the moment I had my first courtroom appearance, I begged God for a miracle.

The district attorney reduced the charge and offered an irresistible plea bargain that I thought was a miracle, so I snatched it up and walked back to my cell-block with a grin on my face. That smile turned to a scowl the moment I heard the echoes from the cell's solid steel slamming behind me. I became enraged the instant my back hit the two-inch-thin, vinyl-covered, cot-like mattress on the surface of a concrete bunk. Rage overtook me as I stared at the four-feet-thick cold cinder-block wall that kept me from being rightfully free.

I was scared.

"Do you trust me?" the still, small voice inquired.

Yes God, I'm just upset. Of course I trust You.

"Then why did you take the deal? Why did you plea No-Contest to something you are not guilty of?"

Because I thought it was Your answer to my prayer, and I was scared. Wasn't it from You?

"No, it wasn't. To get My answer, you have to deny the plea-bargain and plead innocent. In fact, I want you to reverse your plea and request a trial tomorrow and leave the rest to Me."

I went to court the next day terrified, but I did exactly what He said. The judge released me on my own recognizance, and the lawyers looked at each other in disbelief.

The case lasted another six months until it was ultimately dismissed.

"But the first thing..." the instructor's voice brought me back to my recliner, "is for you to get really clear on what you want—what that extraordinary dream looks like for you." He made it clear that in order for anyone to get where they ideally want to be, they needed to know precisely what the end looks, sounds, feels and tastes like, so they can sustain action to make it happen.

Closing the workbook, I pulled out the worksheet to start the homework—to simply describe where I wanted to be.

I want to desire to come home after work. I want my wife to feel emotionally safe around me and to want to be close to me. I want my kids to run to the front door with excitement when I get home and love me. I want it to come natural for Melanie to draw a family picture with all of us together, in proper order with me standing next to Mommy, Ash'Lee, Melanie, and J.T.—not Mom and kids together and me way off to the side!

The ultimate outcome I wanted was to actually love and be loved and have a thriving and growing marriage that produced a united, confident, successful, and loving family unit. But I always reacted in a way that was contradictory to all of this and got the same result instead of taking new actions to get new results.

I chased happiness my entire life. The drugs. The marriage. The divorce. The business. The epic success story. The money. The toys. Oh, the toys...and this expensive home. And now I'm on the verge of losing it all. I can't give up.

The consequence of me *not* taking action registered like never before. My giving up and starting over again on a new, better goal was the equivalent to customers who tear their carpet out and then spend a lot of time, energy, and money on a premature replacement. And of course, because we still don't know what we don't know, we would get locked in the vicious cycle. They purchase a different style floor such as a hard surface floor, and I get remarried or buy a better house, but we both inevitably stay stuck in an unwanted situation for the sole reason that we keep doing the same thing—reacting—so we keep getting the same results: crisis.

Because I truly wanted God's best for my life, I took myself out of the goal-setting equation.

Because I truly wanted God's best for my life, I took myself out of the goal-setting equation. I had no faith in my ability to pick the perfect target. In fact, if I chose the goal, I would be most likely settling for less when my heart was crying out for more. However, I figured if God's past performance was any indication of His future results, I'd be plain dumb not to give Him this task.

"God, please, show me Your best for my life. I want Your vision for my life." Feelings welled up in me, hope and anticipatory joy mixed with a measure of doubt and utter helplessness. I felt for a moment as if I was going to cry, and I whispered to God through the heaviness of heart, "I have made a mess of the life You gave me, and I'm sorry, please forgive me, and help me. You are the Creator, and I am Your creation. I want to see Your vision for my life. Please, show me it in a tangible way, that won't leave me questioning whether it's from You or not. I want Your God-sized dream and Your God-sized process to make it happen. I will do what You show me, and I promise I will do whatever it takes to make it happen. You have my word."

He did.

That night, in my dream, I observed myself talking to thousands of people inside of a large stadium. This was no ordinary dream. It was a transformational experience. The aroma of fresh chocolate-glazed donuts and other delightful treats filled the air. I heard people laughing in the beginning and saw them thinking deeply in the middle. The energy in the auditorium felt sacred and uplifting. Towards the close, I noticed a significant shift in the crowd's energy—people looked empowered and more alive. I couldn't believe what happened towards the end when most of the audience was actually clapping and cheering. And many people stood in line just to meet me. I was humbled, shocked, and flattered all at the same time. What seemed odd is that as I shook each person's hand, I could actually feel their hand shaking mine. All of the different people I met told me how hearing my story and meeting me really helped them.

It was surreal. I was on cloud nine from the minute the dream began until the second it ended. The moment it stopped, I woke up. As the adrenaline rushed through my body, and my heart pounded in my throat, I felt super-charged, nearly jumping out of the bed in one quick movement.

No way. What the heck just happened? Was that really me on that stage?

Needless to say, I could not go back to sleep that night. I just laid there, reliving the dream, wondering what message I would be sharing, what story I would be telling. *Oh my goodness, to help so many people. To see them shift from hopelessness to excitement and action. Wow! Yes, God. That's what I want. Thank You for showing me Your vision for my life. I AM IN!*

When I got out of bed the next morning, I went out of my way to prepare Jane's coffee and rub her feet in an attempt to 'speak' her Acts of Service love language before heading to work. It was my way of showing her that I was doing more than just going to marriage counseling. I was listening to her and the therapist and actually taking action and trying. Unfortunately, she didn't receive it the way I intended. In fact, it actually seemed to backfire.

Yes, God. That's what I want. Thank You for showing me Your vision for my life. I AM IN!

"You did something wrong, didn't you? Why are you doing this? What are you trying to get? I don't trust you! I don't want anything from you! Get away from me!" She crossed her arms, making it clear that she still felt unsafe with me.

Unfortunately, I didn't see anything but the push.

What the hell do I do now? I try to be nice and this is what I get? This is cow crap!

I forcefully clenched my teeth shut as those thoughts sparked a mix of emotions. I felt disrespected and enraged. I lost my composure. "I didn't do a damn thing! I am just trying to speak your darn love language like our marriage counselor always says! You think I'm out to get you but I'm not! You are impossible!" I yelled, throwing up my hands as I walked out the door to get to my first appointment.

I hated starting off the day like that. It threw off my game and put me in a funk. But somewhere, during the middle of the day, I started to remember what I saw in my sleep, and all the negativity of our morning exchange dissolved.

Our evening was strained, but I just tried to keep God's vision for my life in front of me.

And that night, I dreamed again. Jane was there, and we appeared to be totally in love with each other, more than either one of us had ever been with anyone else. We appreciated and held our marriage in sacred regard. We looked forward to spending time together. We were playing catch and fielding grounders together. The beaming smiles reflected our feelings toward each other and the lightness of our hearts. We supported one another and went out of our way to make each other feel safe.

I woke up to get ready for work, wishing that the vision I had seen was the reality I was waking up to. But it wasn't. She was still upset. I was still walking on eggshells. I felt deflated and discouraged. I complained to God and myself.

"I hate wanting what I can't have. We have been going to marriage counseling for over two years now! I have done and continue to do everything the shrink says to build back trust but it's impossible with her. The more

I try, the more I get shut down. The more she stonewalls me, the more conflict grows between me and the kids. I'm in a no-win situation here. Why do I keep trying?"

"Don't give up. There's no quick fix. It's not just a new action. It is a new normal," the still, small voice answered.

The third dream happened the very next night. It was the recurring dream that had originated in my early childhood, right after my parents divorced. The last time I had the dream was just before my dad was diagnosed with terminal cancer, while I was trying to adapt to becoming a teenager. Only this time...in this dream...I was the husband and father.

In the dream, we were camping in our RV at one of my all time favorite spots, Carpentaria Beach. I saw us as a family, jumping over the waves, playing the outdoor bean bag game Corn-Hole, riding bikes, roasting marshmallows, and eating s'mores, laughing and having fun, an occasional quarrel between the kids or Mom and Dad. It's not where we were or what we did that made the dream so good, it was just being together and enjoying every minute that truly made me happy.

My heart sang and then wept as I awoke.

But as I watched Jane slide out of bed, the dream seemed so distant and felt so impossible.

This dream was exactly what I pictured when I publicly invited God into our marriage as I said the blessing over the meal at our wedding reception. It was one of the main reasons why I would not give up on God, my marriage, or myself.

But as I watched Jane slide out of bed, the dream seemed so distant and felt so impossible.

Why after twenty-five long, life-draining years did I finally experience this dream in full high-definition when I'm further away from it now than I was when I last had it? Why the other two epic pipedreams, too? I know You showed me these for a reason. How do I make the impossible dreams You showed me possible?

I knew that these aspirations were not from me or a by-product of my wishful thinking. These were, without a doubt, God-given dreams and the unfulfilled life-long cries of my heart—and God was the One that knew about them best. Knowing this perplexed me.

I was at odds with God and the dreams over the next two days. On one hand, they seemed so real and felt so darn good. But on the other hand, they seemed so far away, and I had no clue as to how I could get there. This annoyed and frustrated me to the point that it made my skin crawl. I was on an emotional teeter-totter. I would wake up feeling excited and, by early afternoon, the hope would turn into confusion. I became irritated because I didn't just want to see my cake—I wanted to eat it, too.

The private dreams initiated a personal mission to find more answers.

I found a vital clue the following Sunday, the day before I was scheduled to give that murky carpet its first restorative treatment, during the pastor's teaching. The cafeteria of Moorpark Community College is where our make-shift church was constructed temporarily every week. I clearly remember intentionally putting on a fake-Sunday-smile to conceal the conflict and confusion brewing inside of me. I sat in my seat, looked down at the ugly linoleum floor that should have been left in the 1970s, and lashed out at God.

Show me what I need to do already! I get that I need to take action, but show me what!

I discovered the eye-opening clue right under my own two feet, towards the very end of Pastor's sermon. The theme of the message was titled: "Why a Kingdom Falls." The lesson that Sunday had three key elements to it that triggered unresolved feelings in me. Feelings of anger, bitterness, and resentment towards marriage, the Church as a whole, the Bible, and the entire Trinity developed as a result of one single Scripture—a passage that kept me up at night and made me question why I or anyone would ever get married. The passage that made my blood boil is the one that instructs husbands to do the impossible: They are to love their wife like Jesus loves the church.

Yeah right! Easier said than done!

The fundamental points he spoke of were love, trust, and unity. "Without all of these in place," Pastor explained with confidence, "and in full affect, even the strongest Kingdom will become divided and eventually fall into demise." My heart shriveled after hearing the words divided and demise.

Wait. What did he just say?

Feeling as though I'd just been punched in the stomach, I slumped over, put my elbows on my knees to cover my face, and held up my head with my hands. I was hoping no one realized how deeply I was humiliated. I opened my eyes, seeing the chow hall's unattractive floor through the tight thin slots of my fingers. When my eyes came into focus, my gaze stared only at my feet, not the floor.

Division.

"John, pay attention to the details here." I opened my eyes again to look for clues. This time I saw things very differently—not from my perspective, but from His.

Division.

"John, pay attention to the details here."

I opened my eyes again to look for clues.

First, I noticed the floor as a whole. Second, my eyes focused on all of the individual tiles that made up the floor. Then I saw my two feet.

Oh my gosh. My feet are in two different tiles. They are divided. The instant I noticed this I experienced a chain-reaction that clicked in my heart. God was showing me I had one foot in and one foot out.

It's true. I'm not giving it everything I have. I'm not doing everything to prove that I love her as much as He loves me...I'm still divided.

I looked nervously to the left of me at Jane. She was in her own world doodling on a piece of paper. Our kids were in their separate Sunday school classes so I didn't have to worry about their penetrating gazes.

If I love Him so much, why don't I prove it to Him and myself by not only believing the dream, but also receiving it, and walking in His ways so I can actually live it? I've experienced His power. Why do I question His word and tactics?

Then the lightness I was feeling was replaced with feelings of guilt and shame. Sorrow swallowed dishonor and tears followed. I felt like a pathetic imbecile, an embarrassment to God, and a disgrace to Christianity. The last thing I wanted to do was embarrass my wife by causing a scene, so I pretended to scratch an itch around my eyes to hide the welled up tears as I lifted my head and took another quick peak to make sure I wasn't causing a distraction. Not a soul knew anything was happening except God and me.

I was ashamed of myself, which instantly and mysteriously triggered in me, an extremely peculiar burning desire to somehow make it up to God, or die trying.

The flame from this new found passion instantaneously disintegrated the feelings of embarrassment and shame. In fact, as I accepted and rose to my own challenge, a couple of passages from the Bible surfaced in my mind. The first teaches about tithes, offerings, and testing God. The second talks about how whatever I give will be given back to me pressed down, shaken together, and running over. The instant I became aware of these sayings in my mind, the experimental competitive, calculated-risk taking, problem-solving part of my brain became activated and supercharged. A brilliant idea popped on like a light bulb in my head, and I put God and I, to what I believed was the ultimate test to prove ourselves to each other. I made a proposal to God. I confided in Him quietly.

Here's the deal, God. I know the only way I'm supposed to test You is with my tithe and offering, but

I need and want way more than just financial provision. I desire the whole enchilada. Therefore I feel like it is appropriate to up the ante. From this moment, because failure is not an option for me anymore, I'm putting more than just a financial tithe or offering on the table. I'm putting my entire life on the line as a tithe so I can test You legitimately.

After I laid out my win-win proposal to God, I whispered quietly and confidently, without blinking an eye, "This is it. Jesus is more than enough for me! I'm going all in!"

I withdraw from myself all of the hope, faith, love, and devotion that I've placed into me and my business, my investments, my strengths, my gifts, and my talents—and I deposit every ounce of hope, faith, love, and loyalty and allegiance into You and Your ways, God.

Here's the deal, God. I know the only way I'm supposed to test You is with my tithe and offering, but...

I made a silent declaration to myself and God and decided to take action that was in total alignment with my intentions right then in the middle of the church service. Without thinking twice, I lifted both feet and placed them together, in the center of one tile. This symbolized two things. The first thing it represented was turning my back on my truth so I could fully unite with The Truth. The second thing it signaled was completing the first part of the puzzle to mastering the dirty dark carpet of my life. As I walked out of church that day, I felt empowered, full of fresh faith, and literally pregnant with purpose. It was as if taking that step of faith to place both feet in that one square unleashed and released me to walk out of the self-made prison cell of limited belief and restricted potential and into an endless experience of freedom and possibility.

I knew exactly what I had to do to get where I wanted to go. All I had to do was the exact opposite of what I had always done. I had to fully engage seeking God and finally, go all in.

The merit of my assumption was tried tested and proven that same evening. The test couldn't have happened at a worse time and caught me totally off guard. With all the lights off in the living room, from the comfort of the recliner, I watched my favorite movie series of all times, *Rocky 2*. Every time I watched it, I always pictured myself as Rocky, as the underdog who upset the champ. The film was at the best part, when Rocky Balboa was fighting for the heavy weight title belt in the brutal bloody rematch bout against, Apollo Creed. With only seconds left in the final round, both boxers had unleashed every last ounce of fight they had left. At the last second, along with the thousands of spectators in the movie, I started cheering wildly, as each fighter threw their greatest knockout punch—both punches landed and shockingly, knocked down for the count, both fighters. An audible gasp swept over me and across thousands of spectators in the movie, who were watching as the official fight referee started the ten count for both fighters, "1-2-3-4!"

As both stayed down, dazed on the mat, countless

prayers from Rocky Balboa's trainer, Mick, his wife, Adrienne, and the thousands of fans in the stands instantaneously ascended to the heavens, and suddenly a tsunami wave of faith infused itself with the ocean of hope and slowly but surely washed over us, causing me to rise to my feet, pump my right fist in the air, like all of the fans in the arena, and cheer passionately, "Rocky! Rocky! Rocky!" As I encouraged Rocky to get up and win the fight of his life, I was secretly cheering myself on loudly in my mind to rise up from the ring floor of my own life's title fight and restore my marriage, family, and business.

C'mon! I can be a turnaround champ! I can do it! I will win my title belt, too!

Then, like a brutally wounded warrior on a mission to marvel in the glory of defying all the odds, Rocky began climbing to his feet to beat the count to win the title, and I cheered even louder.

Tears welled up in my eyes.

I will become a champion husband and dad if it's the last thing I do! I will be the unknown everyman underdog that defies all odds!

"Mark my words. As I speak, I am rising from my own mat. I will become a champion husband and dad if it's the last thing I do! I will be the unknown everyman underdog that defies all odds!"

Miraculously, Rocky rose to his feet to beat the ten-count to defeat Apollo, and the crowd and I were jumping out of our skin and cheering wholeheartedly. As the scene ended, I saw from the corner of my eye

Jane making her way down the stairs. She had just changed into some cozy flannel pajamas, removed her makeup, and put her hair up like she was ready to get a good night sleep after a tiresome day.

I have a hot wife! I'm so lucky to still be married to her. She's such a good person.

I was rattled out of my thoughts and shaken back to the reality when Jane suddenly stormed into the living room. "Why in the hell do you watch this movie all the time? You need to quit trying to escape reality and fantasizing and start making more money! Our health insurance is due tomorrow, and we have no finances to pay. If it gets cancelled J.T. will not be able to see the pediatric heart specialist like he so desperately needs right now! It's your fault we are broke! I told you we couldn't afford this house, let alone a new boat! But you bought them anyways. You never think and you don't care about me or the kids! You always make decisions based only on what's good for you, not what's best for us!"

The negative words and critical attitude deflated the hope right out of me. I cringed the moment I heard the accusations fueled by doubt, worry, and skepticism. My left eye started twitching. Seething mad, I covered my face to hide the disturbing rage I was feeling. I wanted so bad to shift the blame, yell, and make excuses, and tell her that it's because of what she says to me and how she treats me that I do and choose everything I do. Then my favorite theme song of all times, "Eye of the Tiger," came on loud and proud, until it ultimately broke through the toxic energy going on in and around me and brought me back to the moment.

I have to have the eye of the tiger, right now! This is my moment. I will NOT get defensive! I REFUSE TO REACT negatively! I have to keep my eyes on the vision God has for my life and take the right action toward it right now to be a champion husband and dad.

Suddenly, I realized that the Noble Cause I had been seeking—from the desire to feel good, to be loved, to be successful and provide for my family to being on stage helping all of those people—was not it. Sure, I wanted to help people. But my Noble Cause, in this moment, was to be a champion husband and father—to pick myself up off the mat and give it everything I've got.

This is my one and only Noble Cause right now. This is it. All of me. In the ring. Being and behaving like a champion husband and father.

Ding! Ding! Ding! "The new Heavy Weight Champion of the World, Rocky Balboa!" The ring announcer held up Rocky's right hand in the air and announced his glorious victory to the world!

> Suddenly, I realized that the Noble Cause I had been seeking—from the desire to feel good, to be loved, to be successful and provide for my family to being on stage helping all of those people—was not it.

The sound of the bell brought me right back to my own battle. Seeing through the slits in my fingers, both of Rocky's hands in the air holding the title belt up, was exactly the encouragement I needed to uncover my face, and look my estranged wife directly in the eyes, and say with every ounce of compassion I could muster, I almost whispered, as gently as I could, "It's my fault you're hurt and angry and that we are in this money debacle to begin with. You tried to tell me before I bought the house and the boat that we couldn't afford it. Rather than listen, I dismissed your thoughts and discounted your feelings. I was totally in the wrong for hurting you emotionally and our family financially. From now on I want you to know that I will think and consult you before I make large purchases. I won't make "me" decisions, from now on it will be "we" decisions. I'm sorry, and I hope someday you can forgive me."

She shook her head at me dumbfounded, speechless, and exhausted, and walked back upstairs.

My response obviously didn't win me the title belt that night, but I knew without a shadow of doubt that I had just taken a step towards it. This was a first step in choosing right action over reaction, and the next day, I would do more.

The next morning, the worry got the best of her again. "I can't live like this anymore! From the time I get up to the time I go to sleep, all I do is stress and worry!" She turned pale, and threw up her hands after sorting a stack of fresh mail full of delinquent bills. Jane sipped her coffee and groaned. "I hate that we are financially unstable! I can't take not knowing where we are going to live. Not being able to pay bills. Living with excruciating pain that radiates in my foot. I just want to have a normal life. Is that too much to ask?"

What proceeded from my mouth surprised her and shocked me.

Her tone was like nails on a chalkboard to me. It made the

hair on my arms and the back of my neck stand straight up. *This is ridiculous! I'm doing the best I possibly can. She knows I'm leaving for work right now to bring home money to pay bills. What am I supposed to do right now, God? I don't have time to fix this. And if I did, I wouldn't even know how!*

As my thoughts raced with anger and fear, an idea emerged.

I don't know what caused this outburst of worry, but I know I can't leave the house on a terrible note like this. I need to change the subject!

What proceeded from my mouth surprised her and shocked me, "How about a quick foot massage before I go to work?"

She had suffered a freak accident while we were camping and trying to create good family memories per the suggestion of our marriage counselor.

Late one night, as Jane's right foot left the stairs of our trailer, rather than falling in place on the flat dirt, her right foot actually went into a big gopher hole. Her ball joint fractured on impact, and while her foot stayed stationary and planted in the hole, her body did a 360, tearing everything around it. The injury was quite extreme and excruciatingly painful. It debilitated her and put us, as an active family, out of action for over two years.

She was going through regular physical therapy, wearing a foot brace/boot, and still enduring much pain. To heal faster, the trainer recommended regular foot massage to break down scar tissue and facilitate faster healing.

The only person in our household able to provide this therapeutic service for her was me. I did it mainly because the doctor recommended it and because I wanted her to get better as soon as possible so we could start doing fun outdoor activities with the family again. I didn't mind rubbing her foot so much, as long as she was pleasant and reciprocated with gratitude. However, when she acted like a victim, or started down a seemingly unending circle of complaints and negativity, giving her a foot massage was the last thing I *felt* like doing.

It's like these foot rubs enable her to worry and complain rather than encourage her to stand firm on faith! I shouldn't give her a foot rub! Now she is going to expect it more and more! Why did I offer that? I'm crazy. I don't want to rub her foot. She knows I'm about to leave to go to work and make money. Maybe she'll say no.

Without hesitation, she limped over to the couch, laid back, raised her injured leg, and accepted the offer before I could retract it. "That would be great. My foot is killing me right now," she said softly.

Rubbing the injured foot with a strong yet gentle touch shifted her state from distress to contentment instantly. The fact that her temperament changed so instantly and radically upset me even more. I felt angry that massaging both feet for about five minutes seemed to be more effective in helping her emotional condition than actually going to make money at work or spending an expensive hour with the therapist.

I guess I'll do what my mom always taught me: "Fake it till I make it." I cracked a bogus smile as the thought snuck into my mind and then brought myself back to the moment. Still kneading the arch of her foot, I glanced out of the corner of my eye to read the tone of her face and gauge how much longer I needed to focus on rubbing her foot. Head relaxed back comfortably on a soft pillow, her eyes closed, and a peaceful smile across her face, Jane was clearly in a delightful state. Pressed for time and not wanting to be late, I looked at the large wall clock. But rather than seeing the numbers in the clock, I only saw the reflection of my facial expression in the large round glass. As I was feeling used and taken advantage of, I noticed my fake smile had been replaced with an authentic frown, for the reason that I felt like it was more important to tell her to stop worrying and just have more faith than not say a word and just give a free foot rub.

I'm so upset! I want so badly to tell her to stop worrying and just start trusting God!

Just as I was about to tell her what I always preached: "Things will somehow work out," and "Don't worry, It's not a big deal," I realized it would be a mistake. So, rather than speak off the top of my head, I decided to take a deep breath and just relax as I continued massaging.

Lounged comfortably, with my eyes closed, and my wife's fragile ankle in my hands, I revisited the beautiful picture of the true desire of my heart—a restored marriage and a strong, healthy, united, intimate, loving, thriving relationship with my wife. Then I examined the consequences of the two options before me:

I could keep rubbing her feet even though I don't feel like it, in hopes it would advance me towards the dream. Or, I could stop rubbing the injured foot, say what I normally would, but that would make her shut down, feel dismissed, and put me in the middle of my dangerous cycle.

As I reached a conclusion for each path, I made a decision to go against the grain of what I *felt* and chose to try the harder road.

I refuse to cave in to my emotions and react based on my feelings! I must push through what I feel so I can respond with action that is in alignment with my ideal prize!

I beamed, as the thoughts recharged my dream and then brought me back to the moment. It was hard, but I chose to stay united with the dream inside of me.

"Wow, a foot massage was the last thing I expected to get from you. Thank you so much, John," she shared in a calm voice I didn't often hear. "You helped the pain a lot. I feel like I can wear my brace now. I know you have to leave so you're not late to that big job. I hope you have a good day."

"You're welcome. I hope you have a good day too." I leaned over and planted a kiss on her forehead. I noticed a peaceful look on her face and a pleasant tone in the atmosphere as I left the room.

"Wow. Being 'all in' and taking action...this might just work."

"It will, John. And just wait til you see the next step."

I smiled because the still small voice was smiling.

Bring it.

CHAPTER 4

When in Doubt, Rinse It Out!

DIGGING MY TOES into the beach sand, I let myself fully sink into vacation mode.

It's amazing how much I enjoy camping now. It's all her fault. I smiled to myself as I remembered the first time Jane talked me into trying one of her favorite activities.

I wasn't into camping or riding dirt bikes. In fact, before I met Jane, I had never camped in a trailer or ridden a motorcycle, nor did I want to. I love wake boarding and just about anything that has to do with water, but she loves gearing up from head to toe and riding her dirt bike—it's like her baby. Her ideal getaway is camping and riding her motorcycle in the arid, barren, dusty, windy and boring desert with only her close friends and family.

That first ride, I didn't buy a dirt bike and all of my gear because I wanted to. Given my dysfunctional, "colorful," and dirty at best past, and the fact that I'm a self-educated man, and risk-taking entrepreneur with an unpredictable monthly income and ADD, I figured the odds were against me. I was working at a deficit. I bought the equipment and took dirt bike riding lessons in hopes of winning her heart because after dating Jane a few times, I knew she was the one...and I had to move fast.

But man, I dreaded that first ride. I loaded the truck, drove us three hours to the hot, dry, and dusty desert, unloaded all our gear, and got all suited up. It was Jane, three of her close lifelong guy friends, and me. The desert dirt made Jane and her friends feel right at home. Riding their dirt bikes through the brush, over the mountains, and on different trails was a treat—it was like their little slice of heaven on earth. For me, it felt more like a death sentence.

About 30 minutes into the ride, I literally almost killed myself. While Jane waited at the bottom, I struggled through loose sand and then over some medium size rocks and up to the top of the mountain to catch up to the guys. Upon reaching the crest line, I saw her friends signaling me to stop. Next thing I knew, as I was braking, I hit a large dip, flipped over the handle bars and my helmet, right shoulder, and the rest of my helpless body landed squarely on large pointed boulders of mountainous earth and part of my bike to land on my collar bone and ribs. Needless to say, that ended the first trip for me.

I'm glad I did it though. I looked up to see her running on the beach with Ash'Lee, Melanie and J.T. *Gosh, she still makes me giddy, just looking at her. She's so beautiful...and such a good mom. I'm glad I listened to her and bought a trailer to camp in. This has been a rough few years, but this camping has always helped us to remember how much we love each other...especially that first trip.*

We packed the kids and all the gear and went camping for the first time in the desert with Jane's close friends and family. I didn't want to go, I needed to go and I'm so glad I did. It allowed me to see Jane in a different light. Camping in our trailer, with her family and friends and all of us just being in the desert, having fun and riding dirt bikes was exactly what she needed to temporarily escape the hellacious situation that

I had created. And, maybe more importantly, it allowed me to have a newfound and deeper adoration for Jane. The experience filled her heart with joy, and this filled my heart with much needed hope and more adoration for her.

"Dad!" J.T.'s voice brought me back to the beach, and I looked up to see him running toward me. "Dad, I'm going to fill up this bucket and pour it on Mom!"

"Well, that sounds like a lot of fun!" I chuckled as he ran back to the unusually calm ocean to execute the first part of his devious plan.

Suddenly feeling someone's eyes on me, I glanced over at Jane, who was smiling in my direction.

I smiled back at her. *Wow! It looks like Jane is enjoying herself as much as the kids. This is a miracle. You are awesome! Thanks, God!*

Seeing Jane joyous and peaceful and acting like her amazing self again made me want to *give* her love in hopes of turning whatever spark of love was left between us into a flame.

God, I think I forgot how much I love her...like, who she really is...the woman I fell in love with. I gulped back the tears as I realized, again, that my selfish attitude and behavior had caused such pain in her that she couldn't even act like herself, let alone be herself.

Just as I got up from where I was sitting to go join in the fun, I heard her squeal with surprise and delight, and then turn and give me one of those "You knew he was going to do this?" looks.

J.T. had done it. He had filled his sand castle bucket with the ocean water and poured it all over her. Her laughter made my heart sing, and the sight of water on her made me...

Back from our weekend trip, it was time to get back to work.

As I hopped into the van, I started to think about the task before me. *Today is the first treatment of a murky mess, and I know this woman is going to struggle to understand and do the right thing for her carpet. I'm going to have to explain that her carpet has Soil Magnet Syndrome and how it developed. Once she understands that, I'll tell her about my restorative process and how it works so she knows what to expect over the next few treatments, as well as what to do to maintain it while I'm restoring it and after I'm done.*

Put another way, my goal was for her to hopefully set her aim on a bigger, better, more long-term goal—a clean, healthy, long-lasting-happy-carpet that stayed bright, soft, and beautiful the rest of the time she owned it—rather than an instant, impossible target of just looking esthetically decent to get her by for a few months.

In order for her to get the end result she wants, she will have to do proper care from here on. No more spot-cleaning.

In other words, she pretty much had to do what I was in the process of doing with my life-carpet.

She needs to be able to identify her spot-cleaning cycles. She needs to take personal responsibility for the carpet's current state. She needs to think about the long-term goal and implement proper action so she can eventually restore her rug and maintain it from now on.

I held that thought as I walked to the front door ready to start my work. Right as I was fixing to knock, Samantha Smith, wearing her fancy outfit from Liz Claiborne and not-too-much gold diamond rings and earrings, opened the front door and welcomed me inside. After a nice greeting, she began drilling me with questions. "Your estimate is by far the highest, and I need to know your honest opinion about this carpet before I let you start today! I feel like it is permanently ruined, and I should just start over because that is what the other two cleaners said I should do," she frowned and glanced at the carpet. "I was told that it is normal for carpet spots to re-appear and that they are impossible to cure once you get them. What are you going to do differently than any other company that will supposedly *heal* my carpet? What can I expect as a result of your first treatment? How clean will it look and how long do you think it will last?"

> "What are you going to do differently than any other company that will supposedly *heal* my carpet?"

Before answering her questions that caused her stress, I set my story straight.

"To tell you the truth," I responded reassuringly, "I'm not surprised at all by what you have been told, or by the fact that my quote is the highest. In fact, I'd be stunned if it wasn't, and I'd be even more shocked if they would have told you that reappearing carpet spots are not normal. I would have been flabbergasted if any of them would have been confident enough to say they could save your carpet. But I never would have given you a quote to begin with or scheduled this job if I wasn't certain I could help you."

Still uneasy, she threw her arms in the air and took a deep breath. "This is so frustrating to me. Every person that looked at this carpet says something different. I don't know what to believe or who to trust. I'm venting on you, and I apologize. I'm just sick of going through this and I don't ever want to go through this again. I can't take it!"

Her intense stress triggered the rage I felt as a teenager when my mom had landed herself in this very same predicament. *I hate this! This is the reason I left all of those carpet-cleaning companies and started my own.* I took a deep breath to stay present to the woman in front of me.

"It's okay. I would be mad too. But here's what I have found to be true, through research, experimenting, and experience: reappearing spots and the majority of floor-covering dilemmas are simply the result of improper care, not a manufacturer defect. The eyesores are often a symptom of an undetected bigger issue. The good news is the Restorative Cleaning Process I created is specifically designed to prevent and/or repair reappearing spots, dingy color tone, and matted pile, etc., all produced by common cleaning mistakes, which eventually leads to unwanted costly crisis like this. When it comes down to maintaining, preserving, or restoring a carpet, my Anti-Reappearing Spot Treatment and Restorative Cleaning Process are very unique in comparison to what the competition has to offer. In fact, my treatment and process stands alone."

The moment I mentioned the problem wasn't related to a manufacturer defect, I noticed her attentiveness morphing into defensiveness. Because my goal was for her to feel enlightened not blamed, I decided to make the concept completely relatable.

Standing over the original laundry soap spill that initiated her dilemma, I asked, "Have you ever left a little shampoo in your hair by accident after taking a shower?"

"Yeah, I have," she confided. "I can't stand it when I do that."

"By any chance, did your head itch? Or, did you get a rash? Or, did it feel like the residue irritated your scalp?" I probed a little deeper.

"Yes, the residue burned my scalp and developed into an itchy rash. It made my hair feel gross."

"That's the equivalent of what's wrong with your carpet, only your rug's fibers probably have enough soap in them to clean every carpet on the block! That's why I'm only going to do a restorative *rinse* today."

Seeing her confusion, I continued, "Let me explain." I knelt down and drew a circle around the stain in the carpet with my left index finger and acted as if I held a typical finger-triggered spray bottle of ordinary spot cleaner in my right hand. "Pretend that the circle is the initial remnants of the primary ice cream spill. Now imagine I sprayed the stain and then gently blotted it with a clean terrycloth towel. What would happen to the spill? The spot would obviously disappear! That's pretty much a given, right?"

She nodded, as she crossed her arms. "Yep, pretty much."

Never fails. Everyone says and thinks that.

"Is the spot really gone, and if so, where did it go?" I paused for an answer, and when I didn't get it, I continued. "It can't be gone. Think about it like this: first, I sprayed the spot with the cleanser. And second, I agitated the spot with a rag and supposedly the spot magically vanished. But how can that be? Because in reality, if you think about it, all I really did is spray the spot with cleaner, blot the chemical into the fibers, and let the rest dry into the fibers. What I did didn't help the spot. In fact, it actually hurt it." I paused again, letting it sink in.

> "All I really did is spray the spot with cleaner, blot the chemical into the fibers, and let the rest dry into the fibers. What I did didn't help the spot. In fact, it actually hurt it."

"Think about it again from the perspective of the hair and shampoo scenario. Imagine I just lathered up my hair with shampoo and rubbed it in, and rather than rinse the shampoo out, I just towel dried it and went on with my life as normal. Not only would a large percentage of shampoo remain in my hair and on my scalp, but so would a large measure of the original dirt, grease, oil, and dead skin cells because I failed to rinse."

She got it. "That makes total sense!" Her face brightened with a wide smile. "And that's disgusting. Say no more! And to think, all this time I've been blaming the sales person I bought it from and the manufacturer that makes it. Wow, I had no idea! So, you're really just gonna rinse the first couple times?"

"Yes, that is the perfect way to look at it without going into carpet geek speak mode. As I get to the end of today's treatment, I will be able to prescribe the other steps needed to get your carpet back to a maintenance point." I reassured her as I walked out the front door to the cleaning van.

About a hour-and-a-half into rinsing and power extracting the residue filled carpet fibers, the vibration from my cell phone alerted me to a new text message: "Call me ASAP!" It was my wife.

What's wrong now? I wondered, as I put down the equipment to take a five-minute-rehydration-break.

"Hi, it's me," I said nervously, "I'm still treating the lady's carpet with the soap spill and..."

"I can't take this foreclosure stress any longer!" She began shouting through the phone before I could ask what had set her off, "I'm scared! These pushy short sale specialists keep pounding on the front door! And all day people are taking pictures of the house!"

I held the phone away from my head for a second. *We both knew this stuff would probably happen! It's part of the consequences of going through the pitfalls of the mortgage modification process! This is the exact reason why we made a pact to ride this out till the very end! Why the hell is she caving in now? Really! She knows I'm at a job right now! She could have at least waited until I was finished, to unload this crap on me!* Checking the time as those thoughts rattled off in my mind, I felt angry as I put the phone back to my ear.

Still on a rant, voice cracking, "I can't stand that the neighbors are watching this unfold and asking me if everything is okay!"

In addition to the foot trauma not healing despite enduring painful therapy, she found herself forced into what she absolutely despised—uncertainty and drama with neighbors.

Worn down and hungry from battling the residue in the woman's rug, I wasn't expecting this outburst. It caught me totally off guard, and realizing I was now wasting my customer's time, and that I was literally biting the hand that was feeding us that night, I let my temper get the best of me.

The moment I glanced at the text, I knew I'd made a big mistake: "ALL YOU DO IS HURT ME! I WAS STUPID TO THINK YOU CHANGED!"

"If I was there right now, I would be handling it! Don't be embarrassed! Who cares what the neighbors think. We both knew this was probably going to happen! You have to be strong! Don't worry so damn much. It's not a big deal."

She cut me off before I finished, "Maybe it's not to you, but it is to me! I knew I never should have told you how I felt! You are such a jerk!"

Click.

Damn it! No matter what I do, I can't win! She is ridiculous! One hour, she's fine. The next, she's crumbling! I put my carpet cleaner hat back on and picked up where I had left off.

Checking on my progress three hours into the job, the customer looked more confident. She delivered a cold glass of water and returned to the kitchen to let me focus.

My phone buzzed again. The moment I glanced at the text, I knew I'd made a big mistake: "ALL YOU DO IS HURT ME! I WAS STUPID TO THINK YOU CHANGED!"

What was I thinking? I should have re-assured and affirmed her, like the marriage counselor tells me. Not step on her feelings. She's right. Why do I do what I do? What the heck is wrong with me? I shook my head to stay focused on the job in front of me.

While applying the finishing touches, I felt proud of the restorative treatment I had done for my customer and disappointed in the disservice I knew I had just done to my wife and my life-carpet.

God, help me! I'm committing marriage suicide. Why do I keep doing this? I know how to take 'right action,' but sometimes...well, why is it so hard?

God, help me! I'm committing marriage suicide. Why do I keep doing this? I know how to take 'right action,' but sometimes...well, why is it so hard?

Standing on the woman's freshly treated carpet, I smiled at the result. For just the first application, it turned out great! It wasn't corrected yet, but I was positive the customer's carpet was on the right path.

I wish I could say the same thing for my life-carpet...

"Wow! You do great work!" the woman cheered. "So how did it go? Tell me what you think!"

"It turned out well, and I know it's definitely on the right track, but you're, by no means, out of the woods yet. I have scheduled the second treatment twelve weeks from today, and if or when you see a spot appear on the carpet between now and then, it's imperative that you don't treat it with anything. Just leave it alone all together. If you treat it, regardless of what you use, you will un-do what was done today, and you run a serious risk of eliminating any chance of restoring it. For your carpet to be restored, I need you to trust me on this." I cautioned as we shook hands and parted ways.

Now if I could only apply that advice to my marriage!

I drove home listening to a set of CDs by Preacher Joyce Meyer, on Double for Your Trouble, hoping to ease my angst about the situation at home. I knew what to expect once inside the house. I was just confused as to what would help repair the self-made mess rather than damage it further.

Fortunately for me, everyone was already upstairs for the night. The kids were asleep in their rooms and my wife was in the master bedroom watching high school sweethearts getting married on the season finale of a reality show.

I left her in her zone and retreated to mine—the recliner, allowing my attention to wander to the TV show. *Happiness is a joke! This guy is under the influence of wishful thinking if he thinks getting married to her is going to make him happy!*

As if I was trying to change both of their minds telepathically from the living room, I gave a laundry list of reasons why they shouldn't go through with it:

Don't do it! I've attempted everything I know to find happiness! I've tried lying and cheating. Finding it through sex. Drugs. Rock 'n roll. Getting married. I tried finding it in having a child and through divorce. I've tried finding it by coming to Jesus. By getting remarried and having more children. I tried finding it through business success and in making good money. I tried finding it in buying nice things. I tried finding it through reading the Bible and praying. Through marriage counseling and reading books. I tried finding it through doing good deeds for my wife, God, and others. You'll be setting yourself up for failure if you go through with this!

The wedding march song brought me back to the moment. It triggered a doubtful thought. *What I did to my life-carpet with that reckless phone call, after taking her on an amazing vacation at the ocean, is the equivalent of the woman spraying down her freshly treated fibers with a gallon of straight dish soap! What am I doing wrong? Why do I do what I do, God?*

"The problem is this," the still small voice started assertively, *"you treat her with 100% conditional love. The reason you treat her with conditional love is because that is how you love yourself and Me."*

"The problem is this," the still small voice started assertively, "you treat her with 100% conditional love, *which IS comparable to a customer treating spots with concentrated detergent over and over. The reason you treat her with conditional love is because that is how you love yourself and Me. Conditional love is your 'normal' and only way of loving. It's all you have ever been taught, it's all you ever learned, it's all you have ever known, and it's all you have ever done."*

Ouch. Conditional love. It's true. Have I ever loved unconditionally? For even a moment?

Suddenly, the image of my son running and dousing Jane with water flooded my mind, and I felt my heart swell with the adoration I'd felt as I witnessed her beauty as a woman, as a mother, as a wife just a few days before.

> **"You can't give this gift to others until you give it to yourself first."**

Wow! My life-carpet needs what every carpet needs—a few good restorative rinses! That's it! I have to rinse out my life-carpet with special water! But what is the water for my life, God?

The answer came quickly: *"The only Restorative Water for your life is unconditional love. You can't give this gift to others until you give it to yourself first."*

The Truth overwhelmed my system like a bolt of electricity. With God as my witness, that is exactly how I had been *trying* to love my wife but it always fell short.

My heart raced as I remembered Joyce Meyer's words: "Jesus can do for you what He has done for me! He came to this earth and died on the cross and was resurrected to save you because He loves you unconditionally and wants to pay you double for all your troubles! He has an amazing plan for your life!"

Sitting on the edge of my recliner with tears brimming, I recalled that she had been through some really tough times and God was giving her the unconditional love that she had never gotten from anyone else. She wasn't blowing smoke about Jesus. I heard in her voice that she had and was experiencing His love and that her love for Him was very substantial. Hearing her unbridled passion for God and His Love and listening to her testify about all of the amazing miracles Jesus had done—and was doing in her life and marriage—is what had convinced me that not only did I need God in my life, I wanted Him in it.

"All you have to do," she had said, voice rising, "is ask Jesus into your heart and let Him be Lord of your life!"

I didn't think twice, and I made Him Lord of my life. I realized that my job was to clean up my life, and I knew that God would help me. When He did help me I loved Him more than words can say, but when He didn't I didn't love Him near as much.

After many years of God transforming my life despite how unstable my adoration towards Him was, it finally occurred to me that my love for God was absolutely conditional. *It's kinda how I felt about my parents. I loved them when they were nice, but if I talked back, I got forced to pick a branch and get whipped. If I rebelled, I got left at an orphanage.* I felt like my parents' love was conditional, and mine toward them was as well. I didn't know how to give or receive unconditional love. In the past, the only time I felt loved, heard, and important was when I behaved and got rewarded.

As I thought about how I was mistreated as a kid, I realized the rotten treatment God had been receiving from me my whole life. I was a terribly rebellious kid, I lied, cussed, and instigated fights with my family and strangers, I completely turned my back on God, I became an out-of-control addict, I embraced crime, got married and divorced, and got married and made more dimwitted decisions and almost divorced again.

And after all of this, what does God do? He forgives me and gives me His unconditional love, welcoming me with His arms spread wide. This is what you meant when·you asked, "Do you love Me?"

"Yes."

But what do you mean that I have to love myself unconditionally first?

But no one ever told me I had to give myself love first—in order to have it to give to someone else! I was always under the impression that because unconditional love is perfect, only Jesus could give it.

> **But what do you mean that I have to love myself unconditionally first?**

Weren't You just going to love my wife and others through me? I thought that's how it worked.

"Well, that does happen. But you asked why you are doing what you are doing—not taking the right action in the moment—and this is why. You don't unconditionally love yourself, and you cannot *unconditionally love her or anyone else until you do."*

It made total sense that this needed to happen, and that it would make a significant impact on every arena of my life. But why in the world wasn't I told this when I first asked Jesus into my heart? I seriously thought that because I had Jesus in my heart, He was going to love my wife and others—me included—unconditionally through me.

This was a big reason I asked Him to come into my life, why I got married again, and why I invited Him into my marriage.

Boy was I wrong, and the state of my life-carpet was real evidence that I became a victim due to my own misconception—all for the reason that I didn't know, what I simply didn't know.

Wow! For more than eleven years, I've been administering a slow painful death to my life-carpet without even knowing it...

I decided to let frustration fuel my fire to seek out the answer. *When in doubt, test/rinse it out!* That's what I always say about soiled carpets, and it was now going to become the mantra I would use for restoring my life-carpet!

Feeling the criticism and anger rising in me, I became very aware that I was feeling cheated and misled. I intentionally decided to shift my focus to the ultimate goal for my life-carpet—a restored state. My sole intention for doing this was to stay on the path that I felt led to the target, not to deny what I was feeling.

The frustration was an absolutely appropriate emotion, but if I made a decision from my feelings,

I knew I would simply step back into an old pattern and do more damage.

The decision was mine.

Only I could make it.

One choice locked me in the vicious cycle, the other one kept me out.

So, how am I supposed to give myself unconditional love? What does that look like? What does it feel like?

"I can't believe they're getting married right now!" Jane's excited voice, over the already loud volume of the TV, brought me back to the moment with the wedding unfolding on the reality show.

I shook my head and listened more intently.

"I take you to be my lawfully wedded wife. To have and to hold," the man began. "From this day forward, for better, for worse, for richer, for poorer, in sickness or in health, to love and to cherish 'till death do us part. And here do I pledge you my faithfulness, so help me God."

Whew. The vows floated down the stairs and punched me in the stomach. I had heard similar wedding vows many times before, at different weddings. I had also stated them before at both of my weddings. But when I heard them this time, they registered like never before.

As I listened to the pastor saying the words, I imagined God playing the role of the pastor, Jesus playing the part of the groom, and I acted out the character of the bride. What I saw in my mind wasn't an ordinary wedding ritual but an extraordinary lawful, sovereign adoption procedure, which was my very own and officially took place the very day, time, and place I asked Jesus to come into my heart. I interpreted the marriage vows as an operative definition of God's promise of unconditional love to me as His child, and I knew that He was giving me my answer.

As I listened to the man declare unconditional love, I saw Jesus declaring before God and to me His unconditional love promise, fully knowing everything I was going to do long before I was even born,

Dang! Jesus totally does Love me. He loved me even when I rebelled against my parents. Even when I was pissed at Him at my dad's funeral. Even when I turned my back on Him. Even when I made destructive choices as a lying addict. Even as a ruffian. Even when I acted as a devil worshiper. He loved me even as I asked Him into my heart, knowing I'd only use Him and love Him conditionally.

"I take you to be my lawfully wedded husband," the bride began shakily. "To have and to hold, from this day forward, for better, for worse, for richer, for poorer, in sickness or in health, to love and to cherish 'till death do us part. And here do I pledge you my faithfulness, so help me God." Even without looking at the screen, I could see the tears rolling down her cheeks.

He loved me even as I asked Him into my heart, knowing I'd only use Him and love Him conditionally.

"Jesus, I take You as my lawfully wedded Savior, to have and to hold, from this day forward, for better, for worse, for richer, for poorer, in sickness or in health, to love and to cherish 'till death do us part. And here I do pledge to You my faithfulness, so help me God." When I finished, I noticed I had said the words without truly realizing the weight and true meaning of what I was actually saying. I was just repeating a line rather than making a declaration. *I know Jesus knew what I was doing the whole time.*

"With this ring, I thee wed," the groom promised. "And with it, I bestow upon thee all the treasures of my mind, heart, and hands."

"That's a two-carat diamond ring he's sliding on her finger!" my wife gasped.

In my imagination, I saw Jesus making an oath during the final part of my adoption proceeding, but instead of giving me a ring, He gave His life to die on a cross in my place. *The cross of Christ is like a billion-carat-perfect-diamond wedding ring gift.*

The giddy bride completed her vows, "With this ring, I thee wed, and with it, I bestow upon thee all the treasures of my mind, heart, and hands."

"That looks so cheap! This guy is getting ripped off! She should have at least gotten him a decent ring." Anger now oozed from my wife's voice.

Shit! I robbed Jesus blind! I didn't have to do anything for His love. Yet I make Him jump through hoops for my cheap, conditional love. He's right. I totally use Him! If things don't go my way, I kick Him to the curb! When things go my way, I love Him to pieces.

I was saved thinking unconditional love was a one-way street. I never knew I was supposed to give it to God, let alone myself or anyone else. Nor did I know how. I was actually under the impression only God could give unconditional love to me and others.

As I thought about the difference between the two rings, I began reflecting on what it would look and feel like if I gave myself unconditional love. *What would it look like for me to unconditionally love myself?*

I couldn't help but think about my life and just how broken and inadequate I truly was. *I am the most selfish and dysfunctional person I know, but somehow I know as imperfect as I am that God is more than able to work out everything for the good if I let Him!*

It didn't take long for the words to flow out of my heart: *I totally accept full responsibility for my past, present, and future self as a gift from God. I acknowledge and accept me as God made me. Since Jesus totally accepts me for who I am, then I do, too. I take myself to have and to hold, from this day forward, for all my strengths, for all my weaknesses, for richer, for poorer, in sickness or in health, I promise to love and cherish my life and humanness in the good times and bad, as well as happy and sad, till the day I die. And here do I pledge me my faithfulness, so help me God!*

Embarrassed by the first ring I gave to Jesus, I asked Him for a do-over and He gave it to me! Instead of conditionally loving Him, based on what He had done and could do for me, I began totally accepting Him for who He is.

You and Your ways are perfect. You are powerful. You are the Creator. You are Almighty God, You are for me, why shouldn't I be for You? You totally and unconditionally accept me for the person I am. Why shouldn't I totally and unconditionally accept You for who You are? You want to restore me. Why shouldn't I let You? You want my love, I need Yours. I totally and unconditionally accept You, Your Word, Your Promises, and Your Ways, for who You are. As Almighty God, As Perfection, As Truth.

Something shifted immediately. I could see my own faults and needs from a totally different and better view—from God's perspective. I felt more of a direct connection to God and myself, as if I had given permission to myself to be human and allowed God to be God.

If I can totally and unconditionally accept my past and present self's train wreck of a life, then surely I can totally and unconditionally accept my wife's humanness. I can certainly accept her for who she is. Her past and where she came from. And where she's at as a result of what I put her through. Heck! I'm the main reason she is the way she is. I have to buck-up and walk the talk and accept her the same way Jesus accepts me. He constantly loves me in the current state I'm in, no matter how I react! She was scared today and feeling ashamed. I could have rinsed out the fear residue with love.

> **If I can totally and unconditionally accept my past and present self's train wreck of a life, then surely I can totally and unconditionally accept my wife's humanness.**

"I now pronounce you man and wife," the preacher announced. "You may now kiss the bride!"

As I heard the crowd clapping from the comfort of my recliner, I pictured the newlyweds holding hands, walking back out of the aisle united for the first time as a married couple. I could see them glancing at each other with adoration—the same that I felt for Jane on our wedding day and on the beach just a few days ago.

That's it. That's the feeling I want to sustain for myself, God, and Jane—total unconditional love and adoration.

I drifted off to sleep with visions of love and adoration floating through my mind.

The newfound passion to correct my life-carpet by rinsing the multiple layers of soap residue with the restorative water of unconditional love was put to a serious test six weeks later.

It happened shortly after a conversation about building a stronger financial foundation for our marriage. We agreed that it made sense to sell my boat, dirt bike, and one of the carpet-cleaning van units. With the only intention of restoring the financial arena of our marriage, we decided right then to list the items for sale on various websites. We both felt like this was a "grown up" decision, and it was the right thing to do.

That whole weekend, I sensed an uneasy vibe in the atmosphere of our marriage.

By the time Sunday rolled around, it felt like the tension could be cut with a knife. This predicament puzzled me, as the state of our relationship seemed to have advanced a couple steps towards being restored since the wedding finale of the reality show. when I had first given myself the gift of unconditional love.

But nothing I did helped this unfavorable condition to improve. Everything I said just made it worse. It was a no-win situation for me.

Jane held her anxiety in as long as she could until the kids went to bed that Sunday night. With a sad look, she explained, voice vulnerable, "I feel sad and angry. Like always, I looked in your email account on Friday night, just because." Wiping the tears away, she said, "When I saw the three inquiries about the items posted online, I flashed back to when I caught you red-handed four years ago. I couldn't help but feel the same shock and disgust I did when I originally found out you had been messaging people outside of our marriage on the same site."

Her body language and emotional disclosure made my heart race, but I decided to breathe and listen instead of react.

This isn't a new stain. This is a reappearing ghost spot in my life-carpet. I get why she's in a funk! She is at odds because of what I did in the past. If I were in her shoes, I'd feel the same way. I have to accept how she's feeling as a result of my past behavior, even though I didn't do anything wrong this weekend. The inquiries are for the van and motorcycle.

This isn't a new stain. This is a reappearing ghost spot in my life-carpet.

"I couldn't stop thinking about it! So, to kill my curiosity," she said in a shaky voice. "I checked the search history on the computer and found Match.com."

What the heck? Is someone setting me up?

"I totally understand how seeing the emails from people you don't know would make you feel like that." I explained, with concern and sincerity. "It tells me that what I did to you four years ago cut you very deep. Seeing those messages was like ripping off an unhealed scab. I take full responsibility for my past wrongdoing online. I promise I have been and will continue to be faithful to you. As for you finding Match.com in the search history, I didn't search it, nor do I know how it got there. I swear." I reached for her hand and moved toward the computer.

"I know you didn't," she said voice and heart lighter. "You know how they always advertise on the front page of Facebook. I'm pretty sure I accidently clicked on it the other day. I didn't think about that though when I checked the history. I've been sick about this all weekend." She said as she hugged me.

"I don't blame you for feeling this way. I feel terrible that I'm the one responsible for your wound." I tightened my arms around her. "Thanks for trusting me enough to share this with me." The tension vanished immediately.

Wow. I did it— I just rinsed out a layer of life- soap-scum!

When she got up to get ready for bed, it hit me. *Wow. I did it—I just rinsed out a layer of life-soap-scum!*

I hadn't tried to fix anything or even restore the reappearing spot/wound either. All I did was realize that this was an old spot. I told the whole truth and took full responsibility for my contribution to the problem. I re-assured her

I had been and would keep doing my part to help keep us on the right track, and that I accepted and totally loved her, right as she was, despite how she acted and felt that weekend.

It occurred to me that it wasn't what I was going to do that was going to heal my wife's hurt heart; it was the force of unconditional love that would make her—and us—whole.

I sensed a tremendous amount of pressure to restore my marriage had been taken off of me. I was now working *with* God's Love, rather than *for* His Love. I experienced a deeper, more direct connection with God, my wife, and myself than I ever had before.

Little did I know—even though I guess I should have because of my expertise—there was one more lesson I needed to learn to fully restore and maintain my life-carpet.

And God didn't waste any time at all.

CHAPTER 5
Oh, the Phantom Spot!

"HI PUMPKIN, JUST wanted to say I love a
And thanks for working so hard." Jane
energized tone caught me by surprise. "I
on your way home, but I just had to tell y
of the kiddos brought home a super special handmade
present from school today, especially for Daddy! And
I know you are going..."

Thrilled about a special surprise, I cut her off before
she could finish her sentence, "Really... I wonder what
it is! That's awesome. I'm so excited to see it!"

"Oh, I also wanted to remind you that we are going
to my new friend's house for dinner, tonight. You know
who I'm talking about—the nice soccer team mom who
has the husband who I think you'll have a lot in common
with. I want you two to at least meet. They just moved
to California from out of state a few months ago and
their two kids are already good friends with J.T. and
Melanie, and you and her husband could end up good
friends, too! You never know...it could go either way!"

"That's right. I nearly forgot. Thanks for reminding
me!" I replied as nonchalantly as possible in hopes of
hiding my reluctance.

Hearing that she and the kids were genuinely excited
for me to return was a sweet treat, but I had forgotten
about our dinner plans and meeting her friend's
husband. She knew I didn't want to go.

As she was talking, I was working through my
newfound system to restore my life-carpet.

*As much as I don't feel like going, I have to accept
the fact that this is really important to her. She keeps
reminding me, so she must really want us all to be friends.*

155

I feel put out. I feel that if I go, I will be giving her an inch, and in the future, she'll take a mile.

But I realized that if I let my feelings dictate my actions, they would shortcut me back to the losing pattern I had just escaped. *What's important now?* As soon as I asked myself that question, I knew. *If I want to stay on the restorative track, I need to go!*

"Pumpkin, are you there?" Her voice interrupted my thoughts, but the joy in her tone made me feel happy.

I can't wait to see her and the kiddos! I wonder what the surprise is!

"I'm excited," I started. "I can't wait to get home and see it! Tell the kids I'm almost there. See you soon. I love you."

Pulling into our driveway, I thought about the current state of my life, family, and marriage, and the investment of time, energy, effort, and attention I was giving to make it happen. *It's amazing to look back and see and appreciate just how far we've come in the few months/years since that wedding episode of the reality show.*

To my wife, that call was just a normal one. To me, it felt more like a reward and tasted like a sweet little sample of the new normal I was after. I accepted it as a sign that my life-carpet was much closer to being fully restored than I thought. Feeling like all of my hard work was really starting to pay off, I unlocked the front door.

I could hear the footsteps of four cute little feet scrambling to greet me, cheering, "Yeah, Daddy's home!"

I spotted my four-year-old son, J.T., on the landing, poised to fly down to the bottom of the stairs to beat his mom and his six-year-old sister. My son, with a determined yet joyous look on his face, had on his Superman Halloween costume with bulging muscles. Melanie, wearing her pink Wonder Woman costume and super hero tool belt, came racing towards me with glee. And Jane, with a beaming smile, fresh makeup, and carefully set hair, ran towards me. All three were on a mission to love me. It was a close race that ended in a three-way-tie. "Yeah, you're home. We missed you so much! We love you, Daddy!" They all chanted as they clamped on a different limb and lavished me with love.

Man alive. Is this really happening? I smiled ear to ear.

"Daddy! Daddy!" Melanie's voice was excited. "I made you a surprise today at school! Stay right here. I'll be right back to show you!" When she came back, she hugged me super tight again as she handed it to me. "I made it special. I sure hope you like it, Daddy!"

It was another family picture, which I studied intently while Melanie explained, "See, Daddy, that's you! And next to you is Mommy, and that's Ash'Lee." She pointed to each person proudly. "And that's me, and that's J.T.!"

I was speechless. A mix of happiness, fulfillment, and accomplishment cascaded from my heart, and tears brimmed as I realized what was really happening. *I'm doing it! I'm restoring my life-carpet! She drew me in the middle where the marriage counselor*

I'm doing it! I'm restoring my life-carpet! She drew me in the middle where the marriage counselor says I'm supposed to be!

says I'm supposed to be! Wow, we all have smiles, and we're all holding hands, too! It's happening! Jesus, You are SO more than enough for me!

Trying to hold back my happy tears, I kissed and hugged her repeatedly, "Thank you so much! I absolutely love it, Melanie. Your picture means the world to me!"

My quiet celebration of the momentous personal accomplishment was cut short by my wife's voice, "Okay, everyone, we're supposed to arrive at their house in a half hour for a short play date and dinner! Kids, time for a bathroom call and then we're leaving."

Not knowing what I was in for, I drove us twenty miles to our destination. We were greeted by my wife's friend, Lisa, and her two kids: Shawn was ten years old and the oldest, and Bobby was four years old. Shawn was the passionate, focused, very athletic type that loved soccer. And Bobby was a like a cute puppy—full of energy and love and wanting to be a part of everything. As soon as we walked in the front door, Melanie and J.T. hugged their friends and, without thinking twice, all fled to go play in the backyard. And Lisa and Jane walked off without me to catch up and enjoy a glass of Merlot.

Awkward. Thanks for leaving me, everyone.

I didn't follow them to where the party was. Instead I heard a nature program on the TV in the family room and stalled to enjoy my last little bit of alone time, noticing the extravagant interior of their home and the twenty different family photos displayed. I could tell that Jeremy was doing something right.

This natural stone floor is absolutely beautiful, and the definition on that gigantic 80-inch flat screen television is amazing. I can see every dot and color on that tiny fly on the horse.

After a couple minutes of admiring their home, it occurred to me that family and a comfortable lifestyle mattered to Jeremy and Lisa, so I finally made my way towards the backyard where I discovered Jeremy, whose accent immediately gave away his New York roots.

"Yo Dog, it's nice to finally meet you! I've heard so much about you through my wife that I feel like I've already known you a while. Walk with me so I can give you a tour of my pad," he said proudly, as he shook my hand like he had known me forever, handed me a cold beer, and started a guided tour. By his body language, jailhouse dialect, and lack of conventional respect, my first impression was that he was a pompous loose cannon.

My wife and kids had been here many times before for play dates. After seeing it for myself, I didn't wonder why any longer. It was more like a personal resort than a home, and I could tell he was proud of his accomplishments. He had every right to be. Instead of buying toys and spending frivolously like me, he delayed gratification and managed to pay down his mortgage and stay out of debt. I knew from my wife that he had worked hard for it and made *responsible* financial choices. I admire this quality in Jeremy.

> I finally made my way towards the backyard where I discovered Jeremy, whose accent immediately gave away his New York roots.

Through our wives' friendship, we all knew too much about each other. Lisa was a real estate agent and a soccer team mom, and Jeremy was killing it as a personal trainer bringing home over $200K per year. The individual dynamics of his marriage and family relationships were strained at best. Kind of like my dilemma, when Melanie drew the first family picture with me way off in the background instead of front and center, where I wanted to be.

Jeremy unknowingly flipped on an old thug switch that I thought I turned off permanently many years ago.

Lisa and Jeremy both knew about our perfect storm, private kind of stuff about us like the collapse of our marriage, the financial meltdown, my business spiral, my personal bankruptcy, our house in foreclosure—all of it. They were some of a select few able to see each of my wife's and my core beliefs starting to dictate our choices in such a way that began making tangible improvements to the dynamics of our lives and marriage. They had a unique view into our situation. Not only did they know a lot about what was happening to us, but they also knew a lot about was happening *inside* of us, and how we mutually agreed to handle it.

This awareness came over me as I looked around Jeremy's property, taking in all it had to offer, while he jumped in the pool. Catching sight of my wife, I smiled, noticing that her burden of worries seemed lightened as she and Lisa chatted over a glass of wine.

She seems so lighthearted and happy to hang out with

this particular friend. I hope, for her sake, that I can be friends with this guy. I took a deep breath and smiled.

Before launching his floating device in the shallow end, he stood to his feet, made direct eye contact with me, and cupped his hands to his mouth before yelling loud enough for the whole world to hear, "Hey, don't be scared of me, Pal! Come in the pool, John. The water is fine!"

He's got to be kidding. I'm going to drop this guy! Did he really just call me Pal? You better check yourself before you wreck yourself, Pal.

Feeling blood rushing to my face, I shook my head discreetly, feeling my muscles and nerves clinch as the assumptions ran through my mind.

Jeremy unknowingly flipped on an old thug switch that I thought I turned off permanently many years ago. Hearing the term "Pal" immediately made me flash back over twenty years back to my first few days in prison, when an inmate said it with the intent of putting a label on me before I could prove myself.

The thought of being incarcerated in a state penitentiary full of cold-hearted criminals scared me. I was just an emotionally troubled eighteen-year-old entering a hostile environment for men. The first week in prison, I learned quickly that the new inmates who showed any sign of weakness to any other prisoner endured awful bullying and I vowed: *I don't care who it is. I can't show fear. If anyone tries me, it's on! They have another thing coming!*

My intentions were tested a couple days later.

"Hey, nice reps, Fish," a seasoned prisoner taunted me as a newbie completing a set on the weight pile. "Now hit the road, Pal. It's my turn!"

Offended, I slammed the weights down, got up off the bench press, made piercing eye contact with a veteran inmate, who was sleeved with jail house tattoos and bigger, stronger, and more menacing than the others, and remained silent. The tension grew as I put on more weight to do another set and felt others watching our every move. Suddenly, the yard and weight pile cleared because the loud riot alarm sounded, signaling guards of a lockdown.

Back in my cell, adrenaline pumped through my muscles as the door slammed shut. *That chump just tried to disrespect me in front of everyone. He's going to pay!*

The lockdown lasted until the next morning, giving me plenty of time to map out my strategy. On the way to the chow hall for breakfast, I knew I was about to see the troublemaker again, and the time had come for me to put up or shut up. When he came into my vision, I set my intention to make an example out of him in front of others like I believed he wanted to do to me. I sat down at a cafeteria table and waited. The moment he walked by me, I stood in his face, threw him down, and took out all of my pent up anger and aggression on his face and body. As the siren rang, the inmates cheered and watched.

That act landed me time in solitary confinement, but as I walked the hall to my new cell, I felt more respected than ever before for what I had done.

Taking a deep breath to shake off the energy of that twenty-plus-year-old memory, I quickly focused on the sounds of my kids in the background and Jeremy's questioning gaze on me. Fortunately, I was able to catch myself before I reacted to what he said. He didn't call me "Pal" to belittle me. He said it innocently and in such a way that to him was totally normal, but it triggered me because I had never experienced what it meant to live in healthy acceptance of self and circumstance.

I don't want to force Jeremy or others to fear and revere me for how I act or what I do. I just want them to accept me for who I am. That's all I wanted as a young boy from my parents. What I wanted from my friends as a teenager. And all I want from others as an adult. I have to hold it together! I'm not here for me. I'm here for my wife!

Forcing back anger, I replied, "Thanks, I am."

As I dove in, I looked to see if he or anyone else had noticed my irritation. As I emerged from the deep end, out of the corner of my eye, I saw our two wives watching curiously from a distance. The second my eyes connected to my wife's, her lips drew tight. She knew my forced smile meant I was bothered, and I wanted to be extracted from this scenario. She looked away.

"I almost forgot. I have something for you!" Jeremy said climbing out of the pool. "Come with me. It's in the garage," he said as he handed me a fresh beer as I emerged from the water. We walked into the garage, which wasn't included in the original tour. "The garage is my part of the house. The rest is theirs! Go ahead. Check it out!" He nodded in the direction of a metal workbench tucked in the corner of the room, which was obviously his private inebriation zone. In its drawers were different substances: marijuana, cocaine, and an array of different R drugs. And on the upper shelf was a vast assortment of tools to get the job done—pipes, bongs, fat straws, razor blades, and rolled dollar bills.

Uninspired by what I saw, I walked about the rest of the garage and realized his passion for music. He displayed signed album covers and autographed framed pictures. Even the walls of the garage were covered with memorabilia of his all-time favorite rock band from the 80s. As I admired some of the valuable collector items, he turned up the stereo and signaled me to come over to admire his secret stash. At that point, I knew he didn't bring me in there to show me the private man cave. He took me in there specifically to get me high. While I was scouting around, he took it upon himself to prepare me a rail and perfectly manicure a marijuana bud that looked and smelled like it came from the cover of the magazine *High Times*. He pointed to my line of crank and passed the bong my way, "Here you go brother! These are extra special and made just for you!"

> He pointed to my line of crank and passed the bong my way, "Here you go brother! These are extra special and made just for you!"

It was an organic gesture that I actually appreciated

even though I was no longer a user. *Wow, he's treating me like I'm a VIP and pulling out all the stops, like he wants my approval! Maybe I was wrong about Jeremy after all.*

It made me think about my substance abusing years. *When it came to my stash, I never offered it to anyone, let alone someone I had just met. That was generous of him! Yah, Jeremy's a little on the ghetto side, but I bet deep down this guy has a heart of gold.*

"I'm honored by your offer, but I'm good. As inviting as they both look and smell, and must taste and feel, I have to respectfully decline. I stopped about ten years ago. I'm fine being in here while you do it though. Go ahead. Don't worry about me. I still love the aroma!"

"No pressure. I totally respect that! If you don't mind me asking, how in the hell did you do it?" he asked with some disbelief. His question excited me. It had been years since I had told this story to someone who was currently struggling.

"You really want to know?" I asked. He coughed, arched his eyebrows, and nodded. "I quit by a miracle of God! It was nuts, brother!" I said excitedly. He gasped for air as he stifled laughter. "No really! I kid you not! I experienced a miracle! I was just like you, bro. I did drugs to get me through the waking hours of everyday life for years. Shoot! I'm as shocked as you are, even still!"

The amused look on his face turned to shock and disappointment. "You actually believe in God? Don't you know all of that is made up propaganda? What a joke?" A pregnant silence set between us. I gritted my teeth and bit my tongue. We both knew the conversation went flat, just like his euphoric state, so we rejoined the party in the backyard. I was over it, and ready to go twenty minutes after we got there.

Our wives rescued us with a call to dinner: "Come and eat!"

My wife's relaxed attitude became noticeably tense the moment I sat down for dinner. By the time we got back to our house and put the kids to bed, she appeared as if she were about to cry.

"What's wrong, Pumpkin?" I inquired, "Are you okay? What happened?"

"You! You're what's wrong! You're so selfish! I can't even have fun at my friends' because I have to worry about whether you like Jeremy, and are getting along with him or not! Thanks for cutting my fun short and ruining my night, John!" She screamed through her tears and went to bed before I could respond.

What is she talking about? Why is she so pissed off? I'm the one who should be pissed! It's not my fault. I thought I treated the guy fine! Shit, I acted the best I could. I was hoping she would at least be proud of my effort! This is what I get for trying? Why is this happening? I took a deep breath.

As I laid back in the recliner, trying to relax after all the tension of the day, my mind drifted to the job I had the next morning—the second treatment on Samantha Smith's murky carpet. *I wonder if Samantha is going to be upset when I get there. I have no doubt that the wicking has begun, and clients usually get really upset if they don't remember that I told them this would happen.*

The reappearing murkiest spots on the carpet are the result of this natural process called wicking, which has a beginning and an end, and happens in steps and cycles with proper treatment. Old layers of soap residue, from improper spot-cleaning-tactics and cleaning mistakes made by the untrained eyes of professionals, wicks from the carpet's backing to the base and finally, up to the surface of the carpet fiber and, to untrained eyes, *looks* exactly like an everyday carpet spot. But it's not. It's just remnants of past soap residue wicking to the surface and *appearing* soiled. The steps are taken by restorative treatments, and the cycles are periods of time, usually anywhere from four to twelve weeks (give or take and conditions permitting). The number of steps and cycles a problematic area will *have* to go through before it can be restored is typically based on how many layers and different applications of cleansers, the concentration of each different agent, and what different tactics were used which got it to its murkiest state.

It's all good. The wicking is annoying, but it's important. The stuff has to come up to the surface so that I can rinse it and make it look like new.

A noise from upstairs caught my attention, and I wondered if I would ever be able to completely restore this marriage. I couldn't help but ask Him again before I drifted off: *What happened tonight? What did I do wrong?*

I walked upstairs and laid down in our bed. After a half hour of waiting for some sort of clue, I fell asleep and into an exhilarating dream. In it, I saw what appeared to be three future miraculous snapshots of my life that, if I hadn't witnessed through this dream myself, I never would have imagined these as even remote possibilities for me.

The first picture was of a large auditorium filled with close to 500 adults and teenagers, there to hear a keynote speech presented by none other than myself. In the second image was a medium-sized conference room of a fancy hotel, filled with about 150 adults that were there to be coached by none other than, once again, me. And in the third shot, I saw a quaint yet prestigious venue which featured only fifteen competitive go-getters' which were there to be taught and trained by you guessed it right, me, the restorative life-carpet cleaner, also known as Johnny Done Rite.

The majority of participants were everyday people. However, the minority were celebrities, public figures, professional athletes, and even famous pastors from different churches around the nation. And as unique as each audience member was, we all had one thing in common: each and every one of us were there on a mission to stop reappearing spots and restore our life-carpets. They were implementing what I taught and actually getting tangible results. They were ecstatic! Everyday people were restoring their carpet and teaching what they learned and what worked for them to their families and friends. I couldn't believe my eyes when I saw restorative miracles happening to so many people's life-carpet so fast. I witnessed muddled marriages, weak family bonds, and other critical life relationships, fractured or broken, being reconciled, recharged, and restored.

I woke up feeling excited, and then confused. On my way to work, I had to ask, *How was this dream the answer to my prayers? Don't get me wrong, the dream was great and all, but I don't understand how that vision of your potential future for my life is supposed to help me understand what happened last night after dinner. Why do I keep seeing different versions of the same dream? I'm confused. Please tell me what I could've done differently at the dinner party last night?*

With that, I parked in front of Samantha Smith's house, and after our short exchange, my client Samantha with the carpet that once looked like a murky lake, guided me directly to the most soiled section of carpet. As we stood beside the original soap spill spot, which I knew would re-surface by the second restorative treatment, I thought, *Yes! This area looks better than I expected!*

Why do I keep seeing different versions of the same dream?

With a concerned look, Samantha pointed at the original spot and said anxiously, "It stayed gone for a while, but then it came back. I have been extremely careful and haven't even worn shoes on it. Why did the spot come back lighter and why is the color still a little dingy? Is this normal with your restorative process?"

She is doubtful, right now, and that's totally okay. Heck, I would be, too, if I were in her shoes. I know with all my heart that what is happening to her carpet is a good sign, and as much as she doesn't like it, it's a necessary evil in order for her carpet to be restored.

"I know you aren't thrilled by how it looks today, but I'm pleasantly surprised by what I see."

Brows furrowed in bewilderment, she calmly asked, "Really, why?"

"I didn't expect the dingiest areas to come back this light, after just one treatment. There were so many different layers of detergent that I actually expected them to be a couple shades darker than this. The fact that they stayed gone longer, and came back lighter, is awesome!"

My opinion baffled her. I reminded her of what I had mentioned during the initial consultation as I handed my estimate to her, "Remember when I first came out to give you the free quote, before I was about to leave, how I mentioned that it would be impossible for me or any other cleaner to restore your carpet in just one appointment?"

She rubbed her chin. "Now that you mention it, I do remember you saying to me that I should expect the darkest areas to re-surface in some way, shape, or form, didn't you?" She continued before I could answer the question, "I want you to know I took your advice. As much as I wanted to, I didn't treat a single spot that came back. I left them alone just as you recommended."

"I can definitely tell you took my advice," I looked down at the rug then back at her. "I'm so glad you did because what is happening is a totally natural occurring process called wicking, which *has* to happen in order for your carpet to be restored. You see, the faint colored rings that wicked to the top of your carpet? Those are traces of old residue, not reappearing spots. That's why their shade is lighter, and they are circular in nature, rather dark, dense, deep stained areas like before. "

Suddenly, the tension in the room dissolved. Samantha relaxed her shoulders and took a deep breath.

"Now, all I need to do is treat it today and one last time in about twelve weeks. Meanwhile, I want you to do the same thing you've been doing—just leave it alone. I'll show you the correct way to perform interim care, like I promised you, at the end of the final treatment. This way your carpet will always look beautiful!" I smiled and headed to set up the equipment.

While formulating the restorative treatment out at the van, my phone vibrated obnoxiously, reminding me that I had an important lunch meeting with my pastor after the job. The plum line of his last three talks explained the importance and significance behind a believer's testimony, and how we are to share, not conceal.

I realized the power of this when I was first saved, as I shared my original testimony just six or seven months after I became a Christian. Despite the fact I had to fight back tears, people listened, cried, laughed, and cheered. When I finished and handed the microphone to Pastor, he said, "John, I think you have a future in this!" After the service, some of the members said that my testimony built up their faith—an extreme passion was flipped on in my heart and I was never the same.

I can't wait to share my revelation about unconditional love and adoration for myself, my wife, and God. It's going to knock their socks off!

I finished the job, and when I walked in to wrap up the paperwork, I noticed my client on her hands and knees, admiring the outcome from a close distance. As she ran her hands and fingers through the even brighter, fluffier, and softer carpet than before, a beaming smile appeared on her face that made it clear to me that she was well on her way to believing her carpet was actually being restored. Not only did she *see* the difference she hoped and prayed for, but she could *feel* it, too.

> Not only did she *see* the difference she hoped and prayed for, but she could *feel* it, too.

"I thought it turned out pretty darn good last time," she declared, as she stood up and signed the work order. "But it came out way better this time! Not only does it look bright and clean, it feels soft and healthy! I'm so thrilled!"

"You will notice this result will last twice as long as the first treatment. I'll be back in a few months to perform the last restorative treatment, which will correct the remnants of any detergent, and your carpet will finally be restored. At that time, I'll show you how to care for it properly. Until then, all I want you to do is vacuum all the open areas at least three times a week, and that's it." I shook her hand and walked out the door.

I knew her carpet was restorable! Wait till she sees how easy it'll be to keep it looking beautiful. She's going to be even more excited!

I arrived at Pastor's favorite restaurant feeling a little anxious and at the same time totally pumped to share my progress and get his approval to finally testify. It had been nearly three years since my wife and I went to speak with our pastor, back when my world started crashing down on me.

I'm going to be vulnerable and share what I feel like God put on my heart, despite the fact I'm scared of getting rejected and criticized by them and Pastor for what I believe, think, and feel. I'm not asking for me anyways, I'm doing it for Him and them, so I'm just going to push through my feelings and do it!

The meeting went nothing like I hoped.

As we finished our coffee, Pastor folded his hands and looked at me. "John, all the work you've done over the last three years is amazing. You've witnessed many answers to your prayers, taken direction from my lecture, and from God's messages by reading the Bible and your experiences with others."

I immediately felt validated and encouraged, and like it was time to ask. "Pastor," I responded eagerly, "I'm certain that what God is doing in my life, He is looking to do in others. That's why I feel so strongly about sharing my story with you and the rest of the church."

"Unfortunately, that's not enough. The vibe of your marriage has to reflect the tone of your testimony. Otherwise," he cautioned, "your testimony might lose credibility when the audience feels your excitement but sees Jane's heavy heart."

I felt defeated and deflated just as suddenly as I'd felt validated. An angry haze quickly overtook me, and I'm not even sure what I said to him as we parted ways.

When I got to the car, all I could do was pound the steering wheel. *Are you kidding me right now?* The truth pissed me off, and I knew I had to deal with it before I got home. I found a deserted parking lot to cool off and think about what had transpired. After some deep breathing and reviewing my circumstances, I had to admit that Pastor had a brilliant take on it. *I would hate to share this new revelation and be met with doubt because of Jane's heavy heart and countenance. He's right. It's not fully restored yet. In fact, after last night...*

I felt some anger, sadness, and even shame rise to the surface as I sat alone in my car with God. In fact, I think I was on an emotional roller coaster ride without a safety belt! Within a matter of minutes, I experienced my doubt turn into belief, which turned into faith, which led me to take immediate action. I decided to accept Pastor's opinion instead of rebuking it like my past self would've. I felt compelled to do something my marriage counselor often did—I stood on the side of a healthy marriage and did what I felt might best please God, despite how I felt.

This is a perfect chance for me to give God the benefit of the doubt. Shoot! Why not?! I have nothing to lose and everything to gain by trusting Him!

I threw up both fists posed ready to battle like I was the underdog Rocky Balboa, accepting a rematch fight from Apollo Creed to become the Heavy Weight Champion. Adrenaline rushed through my entire body, from the top of my head to the tips of my toes, and I shouted through the silence in the form of a confident declaration, "I don't understand why this happened and I don't need to! I trust You no matter what God, and I totally *accept* what Pastor said as a Word directly from You! Thank You for Pastor and speaking through him, I *accept* and totally *adore* You both! From now on, I am focused on seeking You and helping to cultivate Jane's testimony, not mine!"

I didn't go home upset. In fact, I arrived a changed person, empowered to see my intention materialize. The decision to totally accept what Pastor said and stand on the side of God caused a paradigm shift in my being. I felt undone, as if everything I thought I ever knew about God, life, and being a Believer was turned upside down and inside out in the blink of an eye. I had been repositioned to start working *with* God rather *for* Him. This created a stronger union with God, my wife, and myself. The more I learned, the more I could accept, the more I could rinse out my life-carpet and stay on the path to restoration.

> "From now on, I am focused on seeking You and helping to cultivate Jane's testimony, not mine!"

And the level of intimacy I had personally with my wife and God began skyrocketing.

That evening I had a game-changing conversation with my wife while we were sitting on the couch together, watching one of my favorite TV shows, *Shark Tank*. It happened after all the Sharks rejected a particular pitch that was shady at best. "You don't know your numbers! You've committed a cardinal sin on national television. And it's for that reason alone that I'm out and why I refuse to give you a second chance. Get out of the tank and don't come back!" The final investor said coldly to end the show.

We both agreed with what the Investors said. After studying the look on my wife's face, I caught a glance at Melanie's recent drawing of our more connected and healthier family unit, sitting on the mantle of the fireplace. It moved me more than the first time I saw it. Originally, I saw it as a tangible, unprovoked, beautiful illustration of God blessing all my efforts with His favor. When I looked at it this time, I flashed back to see in my mind's eye the bomb that literally leveled my entire life and marriage, and the self-destructive behaviors of my past self hit me hard.

Yes, we had done some really hard work to get to the point where we could cuddle on the couch again, but none of it was possible without her. The fact that God put it on Jane's heart to give me a second chance despite her desire not to was a miracle in itself. *She has beautiful soft skin, but she is by no means a "softy." Through her eyes, the marriage was over.* Gratitude overwhelmed my heart.

God, I totally and completely accept The Truth that I would not be alive or even free, let alone still married and enjoying my children and wife if it wasn't for You! I don't know why or how You can continually accept me just as I am. I don't know why You Love me so much. Or why You gave me and my marriage a second chance. Actually I don't understand any of it. But I do know that I'm forever grateful. I promise I will do my absolute best and whatever I can to make You and Jane and my kids feel as loved and accepted by me as I feel so unconditionally loved and accepted by You!

I thought about my past self's struggles while I admired Melanie's sentimental drawing. Emotions welled up in me, a mix of humbleness and gratitude. My eyes began to fill up with tears when I realized I had to thank Jane for not giving up. I reached for her legs and said, "I'd like to rub your feet and share my heart with you."

Her brow furrowed softly with concern, "That sounds good. Are we okay? You look sad."

As I massaged the scar tissue on her ankle, my eyes left hers and went back to the drawing on the mantle, and I whispered, "I'm so thankful to you for not giving up on me or our marriage and that you didn't divorce me. Every time I look at that picture, I remember the first one and how I wasn't in it. I messed up so bad for so long! I'm so sorry for what I put you through and that we are still in a financial debacle. It's my fault."

She touched my shoulder gently. "I know you're sorry, Lover. Look how far we have come though." Her face brightened. "Yah, the house is still in foreclosure, but we have a roof over our heads, and we are paying down debt so we can be in a better financial state. Thanks for telling me though. It makes me feel special. I love you and I forgive you. I'm going to grab my cup of water. Can I bring you anything back?" she asked as she hugged me.

She touched my shoulder gently. "I know you're sorry, Lover. Look how far we have come though."

"No thanks," I shook my head, watching her walk away. "Pumpkin, hold on," I sought her eyes again,

"I need you to know that I really meant what I just said a minute ago, and that I'm going to do everything in my power to keep this from ever happening again."

The tears rolling down her cheeks and the beaming smile on her face was a beautiful sign that she accepted them as the truth. The fact she genuinely accepted my thoughts, feelings, and words, made me feel good as I kissed her forehead goodnight.

With everyone else sound asleep, I felt wide awake and motivated so I wandered through the inside and outside of the house aimlessly until I found myself sitting down on the brick fire pit in the backyard, looking up into the dark sky at countless beaming stars.

Oh snap! It's wicking. This is wicking...in my relationship...on my life-carpet.

Wow! I ask for miracles and You do them. My marriage is in good standing and growing stronger, when just last night, I thought we were spiraling again.

"The same way that lady felt about her carpet today?" the voice was smiling.

Oh snap! It's wicking. This is wicking...in my relationship...on my life-carpet. So I should expect this? The cycles of old residue coming to the surface, giving me the illusion that the restoration isn't working, when it's actually evidence that it IS working. I mean, that exchange, the kiss goodnight...it's working. I just need to accept the process and keep rinsing and repeating.

"You're the expert, John."

The cosmic joke of it all made me chuckle out loud as I felt relief wash over me.

This is normal. My life-carpet is wicking. I can do this. When the spots look like they are going to reappear, I'm going to accept the situation in front of me as an opportunity to see how far we've come.

I spent my entire week on the proverbial cloud nine after this realization. Work was easy, home was a joy, and I was feeling good...when it hit me that I had acquired a new and priceless skill that enabled me to correctly identify that it was only pre-existing residue wicking back to the surface much lighter and *not* a spot "magically" reappearing bigger and darker like I was so used too.

I'd just arrived home to see Jane talking it up with her friend Lisa in our front yard. They were chatting happily, while Shawn and Bobby were frolicking with Melanie and J.T. on the grass. But Jane's and Lisa's body language changed the instant they saw my car, and it looked as if the conversation was cut off mid-sentence. Neither of the ladies greeted me. Rather they hurried Lisa's children into their vehicle as if I was some kind of threat. I felt especially awkward seeing both women with indifferent expressions and not knowing what I had walked into.

Clarity came when her kids escaped the vehicle, met back up with mine, and all ran over to me as a team, pleading, "Will you all come to our house for another barbecue and pool party tomorrow? Our mommy and daddy said its fine with them, but Ms. Gray says you may have plans!" Then my children chimed in as one with their friends to close the sale, voices rising, "Please, please, please, say yes!"

Jane and Lisa cringed at the sight of the kids' plea.

Knowing we didn't have any plans, I tapped Jane's shoulder softly. "I'm confused. We don't have other plans, do we?"

She flicked my hand off her shoulder, turned to frown at me, and whispered loudly, "Just stop already! I know how much you don't want to go. I'm doing this for you!"

She didn't want her fun to be my penalty. I felt valued and also selfish.

I'm not in this for me anymore. I'm in it for her! I want to go to make her feel important and show her my appreciation.

I put one hand softly back on her shoulder, and used the other to catch her tears. Pulling her close to me, I whispered, "Thanks, Pumpkin! But I'm about *us* now."

She smiled, as the tension left her shoulders. Then I turned to the kids, "Guess what? We just canceled our plans so we can go to the pool party instead. Time for some fun!" The kids cheered and hugged me.

As we were relaxing in bed that night, she confided in me, "I'm happy you're willing to go, but I want you to know I'll understand if you change your mind. Really, you don't have to go on account of me." It was a gesture of kindness and consideration. I could tell her statement was genuine and I wouldn't pay a price for opting out. As much as I felt like taking the easy way, I sensed the Spirit of God inside of me prompting me to take the road less traveled. I felt as if this was about me and God, not my wife and marriage. In truth, it was getting easier and easier to give Unconditional Love to God, my wife, and me. And I had the distinct feeling that I was being challenged to walk my talk with the very guy I wanted to drown in the not so distant past. I sensed I was supposed to gain some kind of valuable missing link with this guy—one that I would miss if I didn't go. The risk taking part of me knew the stakes were higher than ever, so I accepted this as a personal challenge—I wanted to go for my wife, but now I knew I needed to go for me.

> I had the distinct feeling that I was being challenged to walk my talk with the very guy I wanted to drown in the not so distant past.

I reached for her hands, "Thanks for telling me that. I want you to know that I'm not looking at the party as I *have* to go *for* you. I see it as I *get* to go *with* you. I'm not going to change my mind. I'm excited to go have fun with you and the kids."

I lay in bed unable to fall asleep. *God I know You want me to go, but why? What are You trying to do? You know this guy is a pill and how I can't tolerate people like this. Show me what You are doing, and my role in it, so I get my part right the first time.*

I relaxed, waiting for hints until I finally fell asleep. The clues came in the form of an invigorating dream. After many dreamless nights, I welcomed the familiar scene, which I had been wondering about on almost a daily basis for three-and-a-half years, since the first night it lit up in my sleepy imagination.

I saw my marriage restored, my family strong, and what appeared as a platform or stage with my name on it. This vision was similar to the first two in the fact that it had three similar parts to it. The first two times I experienced the dream, the stage was completely built out, it was massive and looked rock-solid, and I was speaking to audiences from it. This time the final sequence struck me as odd. I was nowhere to be seen, there was no audience, and the platform was only half-built.

The dream felt more life-like than ever before. I saw my marriage and family strong and thriving and each of us looked happy to be alive. Things weren't perfect, but it was evident to each of us, that we had each other's back, and we clearly loved doing life together. I was able to walk up and examine the unfinished stage, from close range. The fresh and unmistakable scent of the raw cut lumber eradicated my ability to reason. Instead, I admired the quality behind the craftsmanship of what looked and felt like a rock-solid, permanent structure.

> As if sensing he had violated an unspoken boundary, he handed me a cold one, and attempted to correct course.

I woke up extremely curious about the dream and got ready for our day.

When we arrived at their house, Jeremy greeted me already half-buzzed, giving me a half-hug like he was an old friend. As if sensing he had violated an unspoken boundary, he handed me a cold one, and attempted to correct course. "Hey John, it's good to see you again brother," he said, as he walked me out to the backyard. "I'm glad you came over. I've been wanting to talk with you again since last time you were here. Do you mind shooting the shit with me for a minute?" he asked. "Let's sit here and chat," pointing to the spa.

I arched my eyebrows and nodded in agreement, "Sure, what's on your mind?"

"I'm just wondering how your life and marriage are going for you these days?" he asked sincerely.

I surveyed the backyard to make sure my wife and little ones were okay and to stifle the look of shock that I didn't want him to see. The kids were laughing and riding their pet, a big pig named Oink Oink, like a horse on the grass and my wife was having fun with her friend over a glass of red wine. I finished my beer and put the bottle down. "It doesn't get much better than this," I proclaimed, as I looked at my wife and kids having fun. "I must say I have no complaints. Life is pretty darn good!"

He looked at me perplexed. "Come on, really? How can you say that when you're losing your house? My wife told me about the sale date notice that was posted on your front door and how scared your wife is. Be real with me. Tell me how it is, really."

Still smiling, I turned toward him. "Honestly, I'm good. I know my wife is afraid and stressed out because business is a little light, and we might have to move soon but everything, including her fear and feelings, are way beyond me. I have already accepted the fact that there's nothing I can do at this point to get us out of the mess

I made. I have absolutely no cash to make all of the back payments and bring the mortgage current. I can't do any advertising or marketing to bring in income for the simple fact I have no capital to do it with. Shoot, we are blessed just to have food on the table and a little money left over for gas and some bills. It's going to take a miracle of God for us to come out of this on top. I accepted the fact that it's not up to me if we stay there, or move. It's up to the Man upstairs. The ball is in His court and so far He hasn't dropped it once. Besides, my responsibility is to stay true to following His message and guidance. As long as I do that, I know my life, my marriage, my business, and my kids are protected."

Every word I said was true. Jane and I both knew it would take nothing less than a miracle to get us out of this pickle. We were doing what we felt was our part and left the rest in God's hands. Personally, I accepted the fact that I had no other choice but to trust Him, so I did. By this point, He had already proven Himself faithful to me. What Jeremy didn't know was that I had been seeking God more than ever, and He was rinsing out my fear, worry, and stress and filling me with fresh hope, faith, and confidence. I was happier than I ever was having a direct connection to God and a much stronger union with my wife, my kids, and the rest of my family. Nothing else really seemed to matter.

Jeremy looked up into the sky then back at me and shook his head. "I'm just going to grab some snacks and another beer," he said as he climbed out of the spa. "You want me to bring you back another cold one and some munchies?"

Knowing I was a lightweight, I quickly assessed the situation outside again. My wife and little ones were content. So I signaled him from a distance with a thumb up to bring my second drink and snacks. My wife came over to see how I was doing. She kissed me and smiled before asking, "How's it going? I hope everything is okay. You seem to be getting along alright."

"So far. I'd have to admit it's going a lot better than it did last time. I'll keep you posted," I said, sinking deeper into the warm spa water, allowing the jets to ease the tension in my shoulders.

"Lisa told me that Jeremy made a big deal about having the spa heated and ready for you," Jane said, kissing me again before turning to go back to her friend.

His kind gesture touched my heart. It was clear that this guy was struggling and wanted more out of life.

Our wives were right. We had a lot in common from both of us going through challenging childhoods, to both of us having to become street smart in order to survive, to being about the same age and married with children. We had both lived "colorful" lives in a relatively short period of time and lived to tell about it. His main concern was to keep making good money to provide financial security for his family. My highest priority was to keep strengthening the bond between me and my wife and children with the goal of loving each of them in their unique way. In other words I wanted my actions to be congruent with my words so they actually feel loved, rather than confused by my inconsistency. It was clear to me that we were both committed to our priorities.

This guy has it all. A great family. A beautiful and secluded house. A spectacular park-like backyard. An awesome custom-built swimming pool with a spa. A totally private and gorgeous $1 million mountaintop view. A stable and great paying job with a nationally known fitness company, full coverage health care, and retirement benefits, too. What more could he ask for? He's got the American Dream! I rubbed my chin and scratched my head in wonder.

"Did you miss me?" he asked sarcastically as stepped back into the spa and tossed me the beer.

The somewhat awkward question and the sound of his splash jarred me out of my thoughts and flipped on my obnoxious switch. "I missed you about as much as I miss old cell mates! No, I'm just messing with you. Don't mind me, I'm a little buzzed and just couldn't resist, that's all." I said, half kidding. I wasn't trying to offend him. I sensed the quickest way to cut through the crap to talk about real life stuff, was for both of us to be on the same page, so I got ghetto on him! It was my covert way of letting him know I could tolerate his antics and had no intention of walking out on him. I was totally accepting him as he was. It was easy for me to accept him as I had been in his shoes before. In fact, he wasn't as far back from me as he thought. I realized, through my wife and brief chats with him, that he wanted to change and was actually trying to change by getting some private counseling. He was at least *trying*. He wanted a closer relationship with his wife and children, and I admired that. It gave me a new found respect for him.

"C'mon, who are you trying to fool? I can take it. I know you're just being honest. That's what I like about you though, John. You're real. You call it how you see it."

Both of us were watching our kids play happily together on an amazing giant castle-like-fort. The second our kids spotted us watching them they laughed at us. Then Melanie and J.T. stopped playing, and suddenly ran over to greet me, while his children remained on the wood structure and watched.

"Watch out, here we come, Daddy! We're going to get you in the tickle cage!" I rose to my feet as they climbed into the spa and tickled, hugged, and kissed me like I was going out of style. It took them longer to run there and run back than the game lasted, but it was more than worth it to them and me! This was something we did on a regular basis. It was our *new normal*. It made my heart feel full.

Jeremy looked at me in complete wonder as they left. He knew about both pictures Melanie brought home and that my relationship with the kids wasn't always like this. Feeling his gaze and sensing a deeper conversation about to happen, I took a small swig of my beer and put it back down. Suddenly, he threw up his hands as if he discovered gold and studied me in awe, "That was amazing! See! That's what I'm talking about, right there!" He lowered his arms and started pointing his right index finger at targets such as his house, swimming pool, spa, and the $1million view. "All of this is just stuff! I don't want this shit anymore! What I want is for my children and me to have a bond like that! Forget everything else! Nothing else matters!"

I knew it. He wants more. Witnessing the relationship I have with my kids gave him a taste and made him hungrier for this than ever. He looked very serious about his goal. *It's simple to do but it's not an easy task. It doesn't happen overnight it takes time.*

"You know what? I don't know why, but I feel like I need to apologize for how I have treated you, brother! I messed up last time by talking crap about God and your beliefs about Him and your house situation. The truth is I had just found out I was next to get cut off from commission pay at work and was stressed out. Before I was working anywhere from ten to fourteen hour days, but I was being compensated very nicely. Now they have me working the same amount of hours for a fraction of what I used to make—I can't support my family and keep this house. I decided to sell this place and downsize, but I'm sorry I disrespected you like that last time."

> Witnessing the relationship I have with my kids gave him a taste and made him hungrier for this than ever.

I reached over and gave him a fist bump. "Your apology means a lot to me. I accept it! No harm. No foul. You're good with me. Sorry to hear about your pay cut, that sucks!" Our time together went from meaningless to meaningful in nothing flat. Somehow something came over him and the conversation shifted. The instant he described the type of relationship he wanted with each of his kids, his eyes opened wider, his eyebrows arched, and he appeared more alive than I had seen before. I knew it wasn't the alcohol either. It was a tangible token of God's power *among* us, and I *knew* it. I was certain it was Him, but unsure of what He was about to do. All I knew for sure was that I was exactly where and how He wanted me to be for what was *trying* to happen. Knowing this quickened me to take a deep breath and press into His Spirit.

"I've got to know! How did that happen with your kids? What did you do? How long did it take to get that connection? I try and try but nothing lasts. I keep taking one step forward and two steps backwards and then I lose my patience and stop trying! What's your secret?" Jeremy's expression reminded me of the hopelessness that I'd experienced in the not-so-distant past.

Two of his kids walked cautiously over to the spa and, from a safe distance, innocently interrupted as five and seven-year-old children often do. The younger one timidly, "Umm Dad. Is it ok for us and our friends to have a Popsicle and go in the swimming pool?"

Instead of turning toward them and making eye contact, he spoke to the wind with a tinge of anger, "You interrupted. Can't you see we're talking right now? I guess, yah, go ahead, I don't care!" As they ran off, he made eye contact with me and grimaced. "See what

I mean! They have no respect. All they do is talk back, interrupt, and disregard! I try to connect with them, but that's what I get. I can't bond with that."

I had noticed that they put off asking him as long as possible. The yard which took my kids ten seconds to cross took his two minutes. The older pressured the younger into asking since the odds might be better. It hurt my heart for him and his children to see their interaction.

He wanted more. It was plain to see. Why didn't he have it?

He's hardworking, motivated, and smart. He's got the heart. He's got the will. Where would he be today if he'd set foot on a different path three months ago? One year ago? You can bet we wouldn't be having this conversation right now. Would he be having much trouble connecting with his kids? I bet he'd have sore ribs and a fulfilled heart from being in the "tickle" cage so much—and they would, too!

While this guy with the wonderful aspiration continued making excuses and blaming everyone else, I was watching him in my mind's eye, seeing him with his kids building a strong and inseparable bond between him and each child, playing, giggling, excited. I saw a happy dad and kids, a success as a husband, father, and person, making such a giant difference in his own life and family, if only... *What? What was missing?*

I looked down at myself in the mirror image on the motionless spa water and the answer hit me. *This guy is a direct reflection of who I used to be.*

I looked down at myself in the mirror image on the motionless spa water and the answer hit me. *This guy is a direct reflection of who I used to be. He wants what I have, and I have what he needs.*

Each of his children were healthy and good every day kids. Each had their own gifts and talents and was completely unique in their own God-ordained way— just like him, me, and you.

The reappearing spots of disrespect, interrupting, and not listening etc., are a result of improper spot-cleaning tactics, not faulty kids. He had the awareness that there was a mess, but it seemed he was taking action the way I did for all those years—Action without Accountability and Adoration. *Adoration...yes...he can't give what he doesn't have.*

Having a front row seat to witness the exchange as an outsider looking in allowed me to reflect on where my old self had started and remember the miracles and hard work it took to get me to that moment, Awestruck wonder filled me.

God, I hated being where he is! Thank You so much for accepting me and helping me get to where I am! I love the bond I have with You, myself, and my family! If I had to, I'd do it all over in a second. The payoff is more than I could ever ask for! You are AMAZING! I accept where You have me. And all that You give me!

I glanced over at him while he berated himself for what had just happened. *All this guy needs is to accept God's gift of Unconditional Love. And accept himself as he is so the he can give Unconditional Love to himself and his family.*

When he looked back at me, he seemed to be frustrated and trying to figure me out. I was very familiar with this look, and I had a good idea about what he was thinking. I looked away from him to our reflections in the water. When I saw his anger and frustration in the reflection, I waited until he wasn't paying attention and dunked my head under the water. I held my breath as long as possible and quickly flashed back to my childhood. I saw in my mind's eye, my past self trapped in the same dangerous cycle, sporting the same attitude and look for over thirty-five-long-ass-years from the time of my parent's divorce until the very day I gave myself the gift of Unconditional Love. As I emerged to the surface, I saw him again in his current state. It occurred to me that the same Restorative principles I use, he (or any person) could use to swiftly restore his life-carpet in a fraction of the time it has taken me.

It occurred to me that the same Restorative principles I use, he (or any person) could use to swiftly restore his life-carpet in a fraction of the time it has taken me.

I restarted the conversation with something Jonathan Cahn had said in his message to America, when he addressed The Presidential Inaugural Prayer Breakfast: "Okay, where were we? Oh yah, I'm going to tell you my secret now, but before I do, let me apologize that I cannot apologize!" I said unapologetically.

I learned as a Young Life Youth Leader and again from our marriage counselor: *Earn the right to speak and don't give someone an answer they didn't ask for.*

I gave him my solution that still burns my brain, only because he asked. "The secret I hold totally responsible for the bond I now have with my kids, is the same secret I credit for suddenly and miraculously setting me free from the chains of my addictions—a sovereign act of God! Check this out, Jeremy. The fact that I'm still married is a miracle. The fact that I have this kind of bond with all three of my kids is a miracle. The fact we are still living in our house over four-and-a-half-years later is a miracle. The fact I'm even alive is a miracle. The fact I'm here, in your spa, sitting next to you, telling you this very story is a miracle. What we are both experiencing right this very second is another sovereign act of God. Us talking at this moment in time and in history is no coincidence." I said humbled.

I wasn't being some holier than thou self-righteous jackalberry. My hope was solely for him to start questioning and seeking God rather avoiding and dismissing Him. I knew if this happened, the chances of God pulling away the veil of circumstance so he could look right at the heart of the matter would be increased. Like my situation, his kids weren't the problem; it was him.

As I carried on with each of the miracles, I noticed less resistance. When I mentioned it was a miracle I was still alive, I noticed his doubts turning into questions. I could see the wheels turning in his mind through his intrigued expression. Yet Jeremy couldn't climb over the wall of God. The moment I mentioned Him, I noticed his look of intrigue changed to one of resistance. I saw that "heard that before" uninterested expression and knew he had checked out.

"I think you're disillusioned by all that God talk," he said with a sneer.

My blood boiled at his challenge, but instead of reacting, I asked: *God, what do you want me to do now? I'm up against a wall. It's already 7:00 p.m. and the kids are tired. They have school tomorrow. And I have to give Samantha Smiths' murky carpet its last restorative treatment early in the morning.*

When I thought about treating that murky carpet the answer popped in my mind. *I'm not here to help him clean his life-carpet. I'm here to rinse it with the miracle water of Unconditional Love. God didn't send me here to fix or change him. He sent me here to simply love and accept him exactly as he is. Man, it's so much easier to just rinse out the soap with love.*

> I'm not here to help him clean his life-carpet. I'm here to rinse it with the miracle water of Unconditional Love. God didn't send me here to fix or change him. He sent me here to simply love and accept him exactly as he is.

I smiled and inhaled a deep breath as those thoughts flooded my mind, only to have the image of that partially built stage flash before me.

I accept the fact there is work to be done on the stage. I accept that this guy doesn't want to hear me. I accept that he doesn't believe me. I accept that he thinks I'm a Jesus freak. I accept him as he is and where he is. And I accept and welcome who and where I am. And where You are taking me.

"It's all good. You don't have to believe because I do. I was just answering your question. I guess I should have mentioned that while God was performing miracles, I was doing a lot of work too. Man, I really created a mess, but I've learned quite a bit about goal-setting and communication and love over the last few years. And all that stuff, I know you will figure out too. You're the type of guy that doesn't give up on a goal. I can tell."

The simple act of just totally accepting him, rather than tolerating or coexisting as a "critic," allowed me the privilege of staying a friend and becoming his biggest quiet cheerleader. It lifted the weight off of me and melted the tension in the atmosphere between us immediately.

The rest of our time together was good. We talked about our pasts, our present, and our future. We focused on our common ground and started a true friendship.

"You have an awesome family and you're a great guy, John. I'm sure you have a bright future ahead of you!" Jeremy was grinning as he waved goodbye to me and my family.

Looking into the rearview mirror of my car as I drove us home, I could see my kids' beaming faces. Jane, sitting next to me, was beaming as well.

Indeed I do, I have an amazing family. And I have a hope and an incredible future, too!

The next morning, I could hardly wait to see Samantha's carpet and how she felt about it. My hope was for her to love the way it had turned out and abandon the spot-cleaning tactics that caused the problem...and totally and unconditionally accept The Restorative Cleaning Process that solved it. As I entered the house, she treated me like a celebrity and introduced me to her friend, Mrs. Jones, who offered milk and cookies and appeared genuinely happy.

Standing over the main area I went there to service, I could see why Samantha was beaming. No spot had re-appeared and the color was still bright, the fibers were still soft, the pile was still fluffy, and there was no trace of residual detergent to be detected. I smiled, turned towards them and raised both hands to give its current state two thumbs up. "I like what I see! Your carpet looks wonderful! What do you think?"

Samantha grinned, looked at her friend Mrs. Jones and back at me and gave two thumbs up back. "Actually, when you first came out, I thought you talked a good talk, but it sounded too good to be true. Now that I see what I see and feel what I feel, I seriously think it's a miracle! And my friend is here because she just bought new carpet and wanted to meet you and get a copy of your free online report. You know, that cheat sheet you mentioned you'd give me today, that's going to show me how to stop reappearing spots, avoid costly crisis in the future, and greatly prolong the life and beauty of my carpet."

"Great. I'll bring back two copies."

I completed the treatment, packed up the van, and brought back two printed copies of the cheat sheet report that I give away online to any consumer that visits my website. I set them on the kitchen table and looked out the window while I waited for them to join me. My eyes went to the green recycle trash bin, and right away I recognized four different spray bottles of house hold name over-the-counter-spotters sitting in plain sight. *Yes, she got it! She turned her back on what hurt her carpet and is embracing what healed it. She has fallen back in love with her carpet!*

Hearing their footsteps grow closer, I relished the feeling of having truly helped another client prolong the life and beauty of their original carpet investment without working any harder.

If only my friend Jeremy could just give the principles of my Restorative Cleaning Process for LIFE a chance. He might be able to believe they work once he could see the great results in his own life!

After twenty years as a professional carpet cleaner and over 10,000 hours and tens of thousands of dollars invested into learning, developing, testing, tweaking, proving, and perfecting The Restorative Cleaning Process I use to restore my clients carpet, I have come to the conclusion that life, like-carpet, gets dirty. It makes no difference who you are, or what you believe, if you are a rich person or a poor one, or if you have the most expensive, highest quality, name brand, or a cheap rental grade carpet, no-matter-what "LIFE" happens and spot-cleaning doesn't work.

The only way I've been able to restore customers' carpets, and more importantly my life-carpet to radical, clean happiness is through a powerful combination of Awareness, Accountability, Action, Adoration, and Acceptance through the natural wicking process.

And now it's time to share the Restorative Cleaning Process for LIFE and carpet with others. Just gotta finish building the platform.

CONCLUSION
A Job "Done Rite"

WITH MY RESTORATIVE Cleaning Process, I have restored hundreds, if not thousands of carpets, which their owners and other carpet cleaners once thought was ruined. With my Restorative Cleaning Process for LIFE, I've experienced more joy and fulfillment within my personal life, my marriage, my family, and other relationships than I knew was possible. Every day, it feels like I hit my life's endless jackpot, which only keeps getting better and better and bigger and bigger!

I could lose it all tomorrow—it's happened before—and I know I'd survive. But there is something and someone I cannot lose, and with that one thing and One person I could start from scratch and build it all back up again in a fraction of the time. That one person is the One True Risen King Jesus Christ and the one thing is the Restorative Cleaning Process for a life that feels totally Done Rite!

I remember the day and exact moment when God quickened me to write this book. I was alone, using my (patent pending) Restorative Cleaning Process, to clean the thirty-year-old off-white Berber carpet at my own house. Half way through the cleaning, I stopped to admire the finished areas. I had to admit, for such a light color and as old as it was, it still looked amazing! The impressive outcome was the result of the carpet mill manufacturing a top-of-the-line high quality product and my new Restorative Cleaning Process, and I knew it.

I looked up from the floor and into the living room mirror. The second I saw my reflection, it felt as if God had placed a double-dog-dare on my heart to stop doing what I felt like I was *supposed* to do—run my business and make money to put food on the table and take care of bills and pay down debt—and start doing what I felt like He had been *calling* me to do: write a book about my journey of restoring my life.

I pulled my gaze from the mirror to refocus my time and energy on getting *my* floors cleaned before my wife and kids got home, rather than paying attention to the thoughts *He* put in my mind about writing the book that would help *others* start restoring their life, too. The instant I grabbed the equipment to pick up where I had left off, the burden on my heart grew unbearable. I became totally frazzled, suddenly aware that this was no longer one of *my* novel ideas for me to just think about and consider like I had always done.

> This was God's desire and to finally get it through my solid skull, He stopped asking me and started downright testing me.

This was God's desire and to finally get it through my solid skull, He stopped asking me and started downright testing me. He pushed the perfect button—the one that my dear mom always uses, *"Your actions speaks louder than your words!"* Only He took it a step further by using mom's saying in such a way that it erased the questions and fueled my fire to the extreme of finally accepting it as His personal challenge.

With the earsplitting machine running at full throttle, I put everything down and walked into the kitchen and shouted to God through the deafening noise, "Okay already. You win! I'll do it! But, just so You know, I'm challenging You back!" I said with tears flowing. "The business and house are yours. I'm tired of worrying, stressing out, and trying to just keep my head above water. You take responsibility for them, and I'll accept responsibility for writing and finishing the book as well as I possibly can. There, I'm going to put it all on the line for You. I hope You are happy. Now let me finish this job already before they get back!"

Little did I know, God had disguised a destiny as a daunting task which I didn't feel equipped to accomplish. As I look back, I can see that I wasn't rising up to overcome a personal challenge, I was actually accepting and stepping into the beginning stage of training so I could start fulfilling the purpose of my life.

After ten years of being a Christian, the time had finally come for me to put my money where my mouth was. Until that point in my life, I talked a good talk, but that was about it. The tips and advice I gave weren't mine; they were from different well-known pastors or gurus, whom I liked at that time. Sure, it was wisdom I was using myself to help me feel better and make changes in my life. They were tips and tactics I had gathered from the books and teaching tapes I had read or listened, too. Needless to say, I was practicing what I preached, but hadn't those books all been written?

"No, your book hasn't been written yet."

Okay, I'm doing it.

I continued working harder at healing my marriage and started writing the book, knowing that I was working on the unfinished platform I saw in my dream—where I was speaking in front of thousands.

After writing for a year, I finished the manuscript and read it. I thought it was "just okay" and this made me angry. The book I just wasted a year on didn't resonate with me.

I saw writing this book just like a job for one of my clients. If the end result of one of my carpet-cleaning jobs doesn't turn out as good as I know or think it can, then I re-do the entire job for free. If my clients are still unhappy, I refund their money. If I don't like the results, I do the same. I don't stamp my company's name on an inferior cleaning result, nor will I stamp my signature on a message in my book that I think and feel is second-rate.

I continued working harder at healing my marriage and started writing the book, knowing that I was working on the unfinished platform I saw in my dream.

I looked at the book through the same lens I used for my business. Not only would it be a direct reflection of my personal and professional image, more importantly, it would also be directly reflecting God's too. I wanted the book to leave a lasting impact. I knew my initial attempt fell short, so I did what I did when I initially wanted to build my business: I found a coach to help me.

I went to a three-day Jumpstart Your Message Retreat to get professional support from someone who had executed what I wanted to do so I could do what they did.

On the first day of the event, as much as I didn't want to, I wore casual business attire, long pants, a collared shirt, and black shoes to match kind of like what I pictured myself wearing as a published author speaking from a stage. It turned out to be a day of discovery, and by the time we wrapped up, I was tired and a little cranky.

The second day, we dove deeper into personal stories, and when I stood up, my new message coach asked, "John, how are you feeling today?"

"Well, I'm feeling better today. I decided to just be me today—just wear my Dickie shorts, a soft V-neck T-Shirt, and last but not least my comfy crocs (my signature outfit), and not need to impress anyone today. Feels good..."

"Awesome. So, you've seen the other two do this. Just jump on in and share your story based on the work you did here," she said while pointing at a board full of notes I'd scratched the night before.

I started at the beginning, the first defining moment of my parents' divorce, and then I proceeded to share every dark and dirty detail of my past. The other two participants regularly gasped with surprise at some of the crap I'd been through and asked questions when they needed more details, while my coach took notes and started mapping a Message Matrix for my book and the platform I was planning to build.

"John, tell me again. What's the Restorative Cleaning Process you use for your client's carpet?"

I'd just laid my soul bare, sharing the story of some of the most painful as well as the most powerful moments of my life that I've never told anyone. *And she wants to know about my carpet method?*

"Well, the customer has to become aware of the real problem. Then the customer has to become accountable for creating the real problem. Then the customer has to take the *proper* action to solve the real problem. The next step is the one that makes me kinda unique—it's the rinse phase. Instead of cleaning, we just rinse all the old soap out and go back for as many treatments as necessary. Once it's restored, the customer just has to accept the fact that in order for the carpet to have a long, radical, clean, happy life, it will need to be maintained using only restorative treatments."

"John, look at this..." Her eyes were wide with surprise and awe.

"What?" I looked over her shoulder at the matrix she was building for my message and gasped at what I saw.

"Do you realize that the five steps you take to restore someone's carpet are the same exact five steps you took to restore your life?"

I blinked, feeling like I was experiencing something amazing but not quite able to wrap my head around it. "Remember how I read the first attempt at your book and told you that it felt like you were trying to be someone else? It was a combination of all of the coaches and gurus you've trained with."

I nodded. "Ya! I didn't feel good about the book either. I felt awkward about it. Like I was trying to be someone I wasn't."

"And do you remember I told you that you would come to this retreat and find your own system and process to share with others—and your own voice?"

I nodded again, still trying to grasp where I was headed.

"John, it's carpet!!! God has been talking to you through your carpet! You get to be who you are—Johnny Done Rite, the everyday carpet cleaner guy. You don't have to be anyone else because who you already are and what you've already learned through your system with carpet offers a perfect parallel to the transformational process you want to share with others."

"Do you realize that the five steps you take to restore someone's carpet are the same exact five steps you took to restore your life?"

I blinked hard again as it hit me, "You mean I get to be me? I don't have to suit up, or be politically correct, or act any other way than me, to support people the way I want to?" A flood of relief traveled through my whole body, relaxing every muscle from head to toe as I let go of the tension that was created by me trying to be someone else. I took a few deep breaths and smiled, "Then it's on like Donkey Kong! This is what I'm talking about!"

The other two participants were barely breathing, watching this whole exchange take place.

My eyes were suddenly opened to see exactly what I was doing that kept me in that aggravating one step forward, two steps back cycle and the exact steps I needed to take to finally break it.

Wow. The fourth step of rinsing does align perfectly

with the Unconditional Self-Love piece that I didn't know how to integrate into my first book. It completely makes sense—isn't the Water of Life also Love? And the fifth step, well, the Acceptance step was impossible for me to talk about without the fourth step clearly articulated. Dang! This is it! I felt the tears brim as I realized what this really was. *This is exactly what God had in mind for me all along— to become and stay exactly who he created me to be: Johnny Done Rite. Guess I still have more work to do around Adoration and Acceptance, huh?*

Once I saw that all the principles, skills, and lessons, I learned from all of my reading, studying, experimenting, and going to seminars and marriage counseling, I started moving with velocity and the healing went even deeper—inside me, my marriage, and my family. I was being more me and letting others be more them, and the benefits of my actions immediately started having an amazing trickledown effect on the other relationships and arenas of my life.

When the time came to write this conclusion, I settled into my office and set aside ten minutes of some quality me time to simply reflect on my entire journey. I thought about all of the ups and downs throughout the different time periods of my life. As I finished thinking about everything that has happened to date, something occurred to me as I began to type the last paragraphs of this book. I realized some peculiar facts.

The first is that to this very moment in time, I continue to underestimate the power of God, myself, and others. Despite the fact I have put a fraction of the time, energy, or money into marketing, advertising, managing, and running the business, my company never even came close to going under. In fact, over the past couple years that it has taken me to finish the manuscript, my company, under God's watch, has actually grown.

The second is that every mistake that I make and see as a setback, He sees as His perfect opportunity to *demonstrate* His power, and to *give* me His Unconditional Love in such a way, and at the perfect frequency, so that I actually feel truly Loved and adored.

And the third is that nothing I feel, think, say, or do can change what He feels, thinks, and says about me—He Unconditionally Loves, Adores, and Believes in me. Period.

It's safe to say that my life-carpet would be further on in The Restorative Process had I realized and incorporated the final two steps of Adoration and Acceptance a year or so sooner. I can't deny that fact. I can only accept it. Why? Because now that I'm on the other side of a lot of my mistakes, we both can see how He has used them and the extra time it took me to complete two totally different manuscripts as *another* perfect opportunity for *Him* to work it all out for *both* His and my good. During that time, He took it upon Himself to

> I was being more me and letting others be more them, and the benefits of my actions immediately started having an amazing trickledown effect on the other relationships and arenas of my life.

divinely orchestrate what needed to happen for me to finally realize I was locked in a lie, which allowed me to stop being someone I wasn't and made me stop building someone else's stage. He actually set me free to be *me* so I could finally enjoy radical clean happiness which became the fuel I needed to put the finishing touches on *my* stage while getting me ready to stand on it. I have a feeling I'm getting closer because more people have been crossing my path, reaching out for wisdom and asking me how I turned it all around. And the ones who are implementing The Restorative Cleaning Process are enjoying the fruits of their labor and already starting to experience the trickledown effect in a fraction of the time it took me.

> He took it upon Himself to divinely orchestrate what needed to happen for me to finally realize I was locked in a lie, which allowed me to stop being someone I wasn't and made me stop building someone else's stage.

When I look back and give an honest appraisal of both sides of my life's proverbial coin, I can't help but see how He has used *every* issue to help me and elevate Him. It makes me see the sovereign act of God giving up His only Son Jesus—who *freely* chose to come to this earth and die on the Cross for a broken, selfish, totally dysfunctional, and politically incorrect carpet cleaner as a much more crazy awesome endless jackpot gift of life then I had ever seen before.

It makes me see all of my hard, dirty, and tough times as a priceless gift.

Even as I write this, I wonder if this was God's plan since day one. I'm feeling like maybe He let my life happen **for** me, rather than **to** me, so I would accept me and my life as I am. So then I could totally Love, Adore, and Accept Him. So then I would join His team and let Him be Him. And then He could set me free to be me and full of His radical, clean, happy love in a world that is anything but, and then start multiplying His team and elevating His name, by helping others do the same.

Whether that is His intention in letting me still be alive today, I don't know. But one thing that I'm certain of is this: The radical clean happiness which I am experiencing through Him and His Restorative Cleaning Process is absolutely, positively the best and most awesome experience I could have ever wished, hoped, or prayed for. I can tell you that if I died right now and never stepped foot on that stage in my dream, it would still be more than worth it.

So I warmly invite you to consider The Restorative Cleaning Process for LIFE and join my imperfect, dysfunctional, everyman, carpet cleaner self and many others, so we can enjoy His radical, clean, happiness in a world that tries to keep us chasing it!

EPILOGUE

A More
Done-Rite Life

I HAVE NEVER received a formal education, yet I founded Done Rite Carpet Care, invented the patent-pending Restorative Cleaning Process for carpet, decoded and developed The Restorative Cleaning Process for Life, and wrote, published, and produced a book. My whole life I always wanted to be famous, yet I chose to stay a carpet cleaner, an entrepanuer, and a student of life. Over my career, I've successfully corrected, restored, and maintained countless carpets. Few every day carpet cleaners have cleaned with more purpose and passion. My secret? A model. More powerful than my cleaning, is the principle driven model I'm following.

In my mind, carpet is the perfect metaphor for life. When it comes to carpet and life, I love both and my goal is to prolong as long as possible, the life and beauty of each.

To many consumers, the only thing more frustrating than a dirty carpet/life, is a recently cleaned carpet/life that gets dirty again fast, and spots that were gone, that reappear in the future at the most inopportune times.

I love revealing my secret to prospective clients and like-hearted people, who ask me how they can restore their carpet and or an important relationship like me. Without hesitation I always say, "The problem isn't with your carpet or relationship. It's the model you bought into that needs to change."

I told people this secret even before I had already published and produced *Stop Spot-Cleaning Your Life.* The pages in each chapter, complete with the five principles of the Restorative Cleaning Process for carpet and life, and all the back stories to support each, had already been written. Honestly, I wasn't sold on writing an epilogue before I lived it.

"Come snuggle and watch a movie with us, daddy," said Jane, Ash'Lee, Melanie, and JT with warm, genuine smiles, as they all cuddled on the new living room sectional sofa, "you'll like it. It's super comfy!" They promised as a movie began.

It was a Wednesday night at about 9:30 PM. I wanted to go to bed because I had to be awake the next morning by 4:30 AM to leave the house by 5:30 AM. On top of that I felt extra cranky and tired because I had just walked in our front door from lugging to the curb for a "special" trash pickup at 6:00 AM the next morning, the most comfortable, accepting, and relaxing piece of furniture I ever had—I abandoned the infamous recliner and I thought. *I'm tired...I just literally kicked my comfy recliner to the curb...Can I at least have a little alone time to grieve?*

Before I could answer their request I envisioned the

recliner in my mind and then answered my question with another question. *What's important now? Staying close and connected to my wife and kids is what is important to me now. I can't be moved by what I feel I need to respond according to the model I follow. I have to emotionally disconnect from the recliner so I can stay connected to my family and model.* "I'd love to snuggle for a bit," I said as I smiled and yawned and began to relax.

The warm and loving smiles each of us had was all the confirmation and validation I needed to know I had made a great decision. After seeing the pleasant consequences of my choice, I felt like the book's content and title was timeless, profound and effective. If a picture can be worth a thousand words, then the content and principles in the chapters can be worth a thousand life-coaching appointments. May it inspire you and remind you that when you see your life as falling apart, God sees it as it is falling into place. Why? Because when you accept and love God and His principles the way He totally accepts and unconditionally loves you, His Spirit will inspire you to stop dreaming about your life and encourage you to start living your dreams!

About John

JOHN WILLIAM GRAY, Founder and President of Done Rite Carpet Care, inventor of the Restorative Cleaning Process for carpet, and creator of the Restorative Cleaning Process for Life, is a transformational speaker, author, trainer, and carpet cleaner extraordinaire who helps people restore their carpets and lives to radical, clean happiness. Value-minded homeowners and decision-makers of commercial businesses utilize his services to easily prolong the life and beauty of their carpet. Men struggling to be the husbands, fathers, and entrepreneurs they want to be utilize his coaching to restore their lives, marriages, and methods of impact.

His credential as a Certified Carpet Cleaner through the I.I.C.R.C. (Institute of Inspection Cleaning and Restoration Certification), educational and experiential background as an Emotional Intelligence Transformational Trainer graduate (Lance Learning Group), and experience as an Ambassador and Area Director to B.N.I. (Business Networking International), combined with over twenty years of successfully operating his business Done Rite Carpet Care through troubling times, has nurtured a catalytic skill set that allows him to identify, diagnose, and help people restore their lives and carpets.

Trained by some of the world's most outstanding educators, powerful transformational coaches, and a renowned business coach, William Osgood, he has tried, tested, and perfected his restorative cleaning processes for carpet and life.

He's on a one-man mission to eliminate high-pressure sales and low-quality cleaning from the carpet care industry and replace it with education-based marketing and his restorative cleaning process for carpet, but his purpose in life is to train people to do to their lives what he does to carpet—restore them—so they feel totally accepted, fulfilled, respected, and important.

John is recognized by many as the country's #1 carpet-cleaning and correcting expert.

He resides in Southern California, as a Ventura County native, and does life with his best friend and wife Jane, his amazing daughters Ash'Lee and Melanie, his amazing son J.T., his Desert Tortoises (Rushmore: 89 years old, Stan: 25 years old, and Lee 23 years old), and the family dog Fifi. He loves camping with his family at Carpintaria State Beach and supporting like-hearted men, husbands, fathers, and entrepreneurs every chance he gets.

A Special Invitation from John

IMAGINE THAT RESTORING your life or carpet could be exciting and rewarding and simpler than you've ever thought possible. If you are ready to get started with FREE ongoing training and support on the 5 Principles of either one of the Restorative Cleaning Processes, then you don't have to wait! We have designed a digital coaching and training community for the Restorative Cleaning Processes that allows you to have instant access to John William Gray and the "restorative cleaning" support that you need, when you need it!

Get Started for FREE!

For Your Life-Carpet

I've developed a Free PDF Guide including a Life-Carpet Audit (life assessment tool that takes 3 minutes or less), to give you a jumpstart on the Restorative Cleaning Process for LIFE along with the same simple transformational question I always ask myself and use as a one-second decision filter that can quickly and effectively catapult you from where you are to where you want to be. This is a game-changer!

For Your Carpet

I've also created a Free PDF Carpet Care Cheat Sheet Guide that includes the 3 simple, fast, effective tips I give my clients that can help you prevent reappearing spots, dramatically reduce the cost and need for future professional care, and greatly prolong the life and beauty of your carpet.

If you would like to experience the program absolutely FREE, go to www.JohnWilliamGray.com. Don't wait! This advanced material is refined, easy to implement, and designed to educate, equip, and empower you to restore your life and/or carpet and realize and materialize tangible results of the Restorative Cleaning Processes without you paying one cent.

This is the answer you've been looking for! Get FREE instant access now. Just go directly to www.JohnWilliamGray.com while it's still fresh in your mind.

Stay Connected

Check out www.JohnWilliamGray.com for Speaking Engagements, Events, Training, Coaching, Consulting, or Carpet-cleaning Assignments.

You can also follow us on Facebook, Twitter, and LinkedIn.

http://www.facebook.com/www.JohnWilliamGray
https://twitter.com/JohnnyDoneRite
https://www.linkedin.com/in/JohnWilliamGray

32413570R00125

Made in the USA
San Bernardino, CA
05 April 2016